Best-Ever Brownies

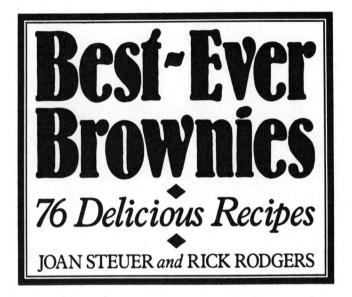

Best-Ever Brownies

76 Delicious Recipes

JOAN STEUER *and* RICK RODGERS

CONTEMPORARY
BOOKS

CHICAGO

Library of Congress Cataloging-in-Publication Data

Steuer, Joan.
    Best-ever brownies : 76 delicious recipes / Joan Steuer and Rick
Rodgers.
        p.   cm.
    ISBN 0-8092-4261-3
    1. Brownies (Cookery)   I. Rodgers, Rick.   II. Title.
TX771.S75   1990
641.8'653—dc20   90-34725
                                                    CIP

Published by Contemporary Books, Inc.
180 North Michigan Avenue, Chicago, Illinois 60601
Manufactured in the United States of America
International Standard Book Number: 0-8092-4261-3

CONTENTS

WHAT MAKES A BROWNIE THE BEST EVER?

We define the "best-ever brownie" as moist and rich with pronounced deep chocolate flavor. It is dense and fudgy in the center, but never wet. The edges are chewy, but never dry. The brownie has a slightly shiny top with few, if any, cracks.

ACKNOWLEDGMENTS

The authors would like to thank the following friends and collegues for their donations of recipes, product, emotional support and/or waistlines—all in the name of Chocolate: Barbara Albright, Flo Braker, Rose Levy Berenbaum, Irena Chalmers, Beth Hensperger, Diane Kniss, Michael McLaughlin, Beverly Moody, Betty Rosbottom, Richard Sax and Lisa Van Riper of Fleishmann-Hillard for Hershey's Cocoa. A special tip of the toque to Adrienne Welch.

PREFACE

Everyone loves brownies. And brownies are indeed lovable. We think brownies are the best "good mood" food we know. After all, we can always count on a fresh batch of dense, rich, fudgy brownies to make us feel good. Licking the spoon evokes memories of helping Mom in the kitchen, and, as the aroma of baking brownies wafts through the house, we feel comforted. Yet, only after taste testing hundreds of brownies—from healthful whole wheat 'n' honey types to decadent chocolate brownie chunk cheesecake—did we discover that rather than sample every brownie we could find, we wanted to indulge only in the best.

We tried to create batches of traditional fudgy, chewy, and cakey brownies that are chocolaty rich instead of sugary sweet. We have chosen our favorite flavors to combine with chocolate and developed moist Gingered Applesauce Brownies, chewy P.B. Peanut-Butter Frosted Brownies, and Cappuccino Frozen Yogurt Brownie Pie.

In the course of writing this book, nearly everyone we spoke to had "the best brownie recipe," and as we ran out of pages before we ran out of recipes, we may have been unable to include your personal favorite. We hope you'll forgive us, as we wanted to add a few extraordinary and unique brownie-derived desserts such as a bittersweet orange-scented Valencia Brownie Torte, a Brownie Soufflé with Brandied Chocolate Sauce, and a Chocolate Brownie Fruit Tart, just in case our more simple all-American squares of chocolaty inspiration fail to excite you.

Whether you prefer your brownies dense, fudgy, and slightly wet, chewy and moist, or cakey and light, we hope we've helped to make your next brownie experience the Best-Ever.

A BRIEF HISTORICAL PERSPECTIVE OR THE ORIGIN OF THE BROWNIE

Webster defines the edible brownie as "a small square or rectangle of rich cake, usually chocolate, often containing nuts." Surely we must agree that a brownie is not simply a piece of cake.

As to the origin of the brownie, one legend claims that a clumsy baker dropped a chocolate cake, creating a much adored, but very condensed, flat chocolate cake. Most cookbooks, however, favor the theory that our favorite chocolate snack and dessert was named for its characteristic deep-brown color, yet one of the earliest brownie recipes ever written appears in the original 1896 version of the *Fanny Farmer Cookbook* and doesn't contain a trace of chocolate.

Though the origin of the brownie remains questionable, brownies have been American favorites since the nineteenth century. Today's variations on a theme feature novel brownie items, such as frozen brownies-on-a-stick, microwaveable brownies, and "healthy" oat-bran, or fruit-and-nut brownies. We, however, still like ours the old-fashioned way—chocolate.

Part I
THE BASICS

1
INTRODUCTION AND TYPES OF CHOCOLATE

MAKING YOUR BROWNIES "THE BEST EVER"

Fudgy, chewy, or cakey, studded with nuts or chock-full of chocolate, brownies are traditionally easy to prepare. Yet even for the most basic baking tasks, there are a few simple tricks that will ensure more successful results. After baking literally hundreds of different brownies, we have developed a list of suggestions and tips that can be used to improve most brownie recipes, be it from our book or your own collection.

A FEW WORDS ON CHOCOLATE

Understanding chocolate can be vital to brownie-baking success. Although each brand of chocolate is made from a proprietary blend of cacao beans, there are several Standards of Identity or FDA definitions for the various types of chocolate.

UNSWEETENED CHOCOLATE

Unsweetened chocolate is pure chocolate liquor that has been cooled and molded into blocks. The base of all chocolate products, chocolate liquor is the rich, dark-brown, fluid mass made by grinding the nibs of cacao beans. It is also known as *baking* or *bitter chocolate*. The cocoa butter content ranges from 50 to 58 percent, averaging about 53 percent. Unsweetened chocolate is palatable but not very tasty. Its flavor is based on the quality and variety of cacao beans used, the acid content of the beans, and the blending, roasting, and refining processes. This is the type of chocolate most frequently used in brownies.

UNSWEETENED COCOA POWDER

Cocoa powder is pure chocolate liquor with 75 percent of the cocoa butter removed.

Natural cocoa powder or *nonalkalized cocoa powder* generally has a stronger chocolate flavor than *alkalized cocoa powder*, also known as *Dutch-processed cocoa*, which has been treated with an alkali to make the cocoa more soluble and neutralize its natural acidity. Alkalized cocoa is darker in color, but has a milder flavor, than natural cocoa. Most imported cocoa powders are alkalized.

Since most of our recipes call for baking soda (an alkali) as the leavening agent, we generally use natural, nonalkalized cocoa, which is acidic and gives a slightly stronger chocolate flavor. In recipes which do not specify a type of cocoa powder, either may be used.

SWEET CHOCOLATE AND SEMISWEET CHOCOLATE

Sweet chocolate must contain at least 15 percent chocolate liquor and generally has a higher percentage of sugar than bittersweet or semisweet chocolates.

Bittersweet and *semisweet chocolate* are alternate names for sweet chocolate that contains at least 35 percent chocolate liquor. Although both semisweet and bittersweet chocolate fall under the same classification, the degree of chocolate flavor and sweetness varies dramatically among different brands in this category.

MILK CHOCOLATE

America's favorite eating chocolate, milk chocolate must contain at least 10 percent chocolate liquor, 3.66 percent milk fat, and at least 12 percent milk solids. The texture of milk chocolate is softer than that of dark (unsweetened and sweet) chocolate, and the chocolate flavor is generally milder.

WHITE CHOCOLATE

White chocolate has no chocolate liquor and is not considered "real chocolate" by U.S. standards. High-quality white chocolate is usually ivory in color and is made from cocoa butter, sugar, milk solids, lecithin, and vanilla or vanillin. Cocoa butter imparts a faint chocolaty aroma, sweet taste, and creamy texture. When shopping for white chocolate, do check the label for cocoa butter.

We use the following chocolates for all recipes in this book:

Baker's German's Sweet Chocolate
Baker's Semisweet Chocolate
Baker's Unsweetened Chocolate
Lindt Excellence Bittersweet Chocolate
Droste Cocoa Powder (for recipes calling for alkalized cocoa powder)
Hershey's Cocoa Powder (for recipes calling for nonalkalized cocoa powder)
Lindt Blancor "White Chocolate" (also labeled Lindt Blanc Swiss
　　Confectionary Bar)
Tobler Milk Chocolate

We recommend using these brands of chocolate when re-creating our recipes, as substitutions may cause variations in texture, baking times, appearance, and flavor. Of course, you may use other brands of chocolate, if necessary, but do *not* simply substitute different types of chocolate—for example, semisweet chocolate for unsweetened chocolate—adjust the amount of sugar, and assume the recipe will work. We've tried and can assure you that chances are it *won't* work. One brand's semisweet may be another brand's bittersweet. In fact, as there is no industry standard for the amount of sugar in the various types of chocolate containing sugar, one brand's bittersweet chocolate may actually be sweeter and have a milder chocolate flavor than another brand's semisweet chocolate. Clearly, substitutions can be risky, and the flavor of the brownie will certainly be affected. In recipes calling for *semisweet or bittersweet chocolate*, we have tested the recipes with both types of chocolate.

2
BASIC CHOCOLATE TECHNIQUES

CHOPPING CHOCOLATE

Chopping chocolate properly will ensure smooth and speedy melting. As a rule of thumb, remember that the greater the surface area, the more uniform the melt. Therefore, finely chopped chocolate spread over the bottom of a double boiler will melt more quickly and evenly than large, unchopped pieces. We define *finely chopped chocolate* as pieces less than ¼-inch square, and it is most suitable for melting. *Coarsely chopped chocolate* is chopped into pieces ½-inch square and is generally used for chunks in a batter.

A large, sharp chef's knife is best for chopping chocolate. Use a dry, odor-free cutting surface, preferably plastic. If possible, have two separate chopping boards in your kitchen—one for sweet ingredients (chocolate, nuts, dried fruits) and one for savory (garlic, onions, and herbs). This will prevent garlic-flavored brownies. Generally, we do not recommend chopping chocolate in a food processor, as it may melt from the resulting friction. (We have included one recipe for a special fudgy brownie exception in which a food processor is sucessfully used to chop chocolate; see Barb's Fudgy Food-Processor Brownies in Index.)

MELTING CHOCOLATE

There are several basic methods of melting chocolate. The first method is used specifically for brownie recipes calling for melting chocolate and butter together.

Method One: Although many standard brownie recipes may direct you to melt chocolate and butter together over low heat, melting chocolate over direct heat of any intensity can easily cause scorching. Also, at temperatures above 120°F, chocolate may begin to lose its flavor. Based on extensive experiments with alternative melting techniques, we feel the following method works best. *In a medium saucepan over low heat, heat the butter until it is just melted but not sizzling. Remove the pan from the heat and add the finely chopped chocolate. Let the mixture stand for a minute or two; the residual heat from the saucepan will gently melt the chocolate. Whisk the butter and chocolate together until smooth.* Don't worry if you have a few unmelted pieces of chocolate left, as they will melt completely during the subsequent standing period. Be sure to let the chocolate-butter mixture cool for about 10 minutes or so, until it is at least tepid. If you proceed immediately, using a hot mixture, your brownies may turn out dry. You can use this method in any brownie recipe that calls for melting butter and chocolate together.

The following traditional double-boiler method and the more modern microwave version are usually used to melt chocolate only. When using either of these methods, melt the chocolate uncovered, so that no condensed beads of moisture will drip into the chocolate. Overheated chocolate "seizes" or becomes very thick and grainy. You can try to correct this problem by adding 1 teaspoon of solid vegetable shortening (not butter or margarine) for every 2 ounces of melted chocolate and stirring until smooth.

Method Two: For the double-boiler method, heat the finely chopped chocolate in the top of an uncovered double boiler over very hot, not simmering, water, stirring occasionally until it is melted and smooth. Milk and white chocolates have high proportions of milk proteins, butter fats, and sugar that clump and burn easily and are melted most successfully if hot tap water (not above 125°F) touches the bottom of the double-boiler insert. Stir milk and white chocolate very often to avoid clumping.

Method Three: For the microwave method, place the finely chopped chocolate in a microwave-proof bowl and microwave at 50 percent energy for 2 to 4 minutes, interrupting the procedure about every 30 seconds to stir. The chocolate may not always appear melted and should be stirred until smooth.

STORING CHOCOLATE

Chocolate should be stored properly for optimal brownie-baking results. Wrap all types of chocolate in aluminum foil, then plastic wrap, to provide a barrier to moisture, light, and foreign odors. Store in a cool, dry place with good ventilation, out of direct sunlight. Ideal storage temperatures range from 60°F to 75°F, with less than 50 percent humidity.

3
OTHER INGREDIENTS

BUTTER

Unsalted butter, or sweet butter, is used in all recipes. If using salted butter, decrease any salt in the recipe to taste. To soften cold butter quickly for creaming purposes, grate the butter coarsely into a bowl, then proceed with the recipe. Or, you may soften an unwrapped portion of butter, cut into pieces, in the microwave at low (10 percent) power. Allow about 1 minute for a 4-ounce stick (8 tablespoons) to soften. The butter should be barely softened and pliable, not shiny and greasy.

EGGS

USDA grade A large eggs are used in all recipes. If a recipe calls for using eggs at room temperature, you may quickly bring the eggs to the proper temperature by placing chilled, unbroken eggs in a bowl filled with hot tap water and letting them stand for 5 minutes.

FLOUR

All-purpose flour is used in all recipes, unless otherwise specified. Measure flour by the dip-and-scoop method: dip your measuring cup into the bag or canister of flour and level off the top with a knife.

NUTS

Toasting enhances the flavor of nuts and adds textural variation to chewy, fudgy, and cakelike brownies.

To toast almonds, pecans, walnuts, and hazelnuts, place the nuts in a single layer on a baking sheet and bake them in a preheated 350°F oven for 8 to 10 minutes, shaking the pan a couple of times, until the nuts are lightly browned and fragrant. (Note: Macadamia nuts will take slightly less time.) Let them cool completely before chopping.

To skin hazelnuts, wrap the toasted, warm hazelnuts in a clean kitchen towel and let them stand for 20 minutes. Using the towel, rub off the skins. Stubborn skins can be removed by rubbing the hazelnuts against a fine-meshed wire sieve.

Some recipes call for unsalted cashews, peanuts, or macadamia nuts, which are generally found in salted versions (though they are available unsalted in health-food stores). To remove salt, place the nuts in a wire sieve and rinse them completely under cold running water. Drain them well and pat dry with paper towels.

SUGAR

Granulated sugar is used in most recipes. In recipes calling for brown sugar, we use light brown sugar. Although dark brown sugar has slightly more molasses in it, light and dark brown sugars can generally be interchanged with little difference in taste and appearance in the final brownie.

4
EQUIPMENT

BAKING PANS

The specific size of the pan used is very important. Most of our recipes call for 8- or 9-inch square pans, although some larger-sized batches will call for a 9″ × 13″ rectangular pan, a 10″ × 15″ or 11″ × 17″ jelly-roll pan. When in doubt, measure the bottom of your pan from side to side. If you use glass baking dishes, decrease the oven temperature by 25°F and the baking time by 5 minutes.

ELECTRIC MIXERS

All recipes have been tested using a hand-held electric mixer. You may use a standing heavy-duty mixer, but reduce mixing times slightly to compensate for the increased power. Use the visual descriptions in the recipes as guidelines. If you use a mixer to beat dry ingredients into a batter, beat on low speed, just until dry ingredients are incorporated. *Never overbeat a brownie batter, or your brownies will be coarse and dry.*

FOOD PROCESSOR

The food processor, while excellent for chopping nuts and grinding cookies or crackers for crusts, is generally not recommended for chopping chocolate.

5
TYPES OF BROWNIES

There are three basic types of brownies: fudgy, chewy, and cakey. To help readers with specific textural preferences, each brownie recipe in this book is labeled according to the following definitions:

 FUDGY

This classic brownie has the flavor and texture we all grew up with. It is gooey (almost wet) in the middle, with a shiny, flaky top and rich, intense chocolate flavor. The traditional fudgy brownie is made with unsweetened chocolate and is heavy and sweet with a full, slightly harsh chocolate flavor. The precise ratio of ingredients is critical to baking successful fudgy brownies. Fudgy brownies are usually made with melted butter, extra sugar, and very little flour.

 CHEWY

Chewy brownies are soft and moist and yield a slight toothsome tug in every bite. Generally thicker than fudgy brownies, chewy brownies are slightly crusty on the edges and the top without being crumbly. Chewy chocolate brownies are often made with bittersweet or semisweet chocolate and have a milder chocolate flavor than fudgy brownies. A combination of light brown sugar and corn syrup often replaces granulated sugar to create moister, chewier brownies. Creamed butter also adds volume to the brownie batter, directly affecting the finished result.

 CAKEY

Cakey brownies have a moist, light crumb and a smooth, barely discernible top. The texture is often springy to the touch, and the flavor varies from deep, dark, and chocolaty to light, subtle, and mild. This brownie often closely resembles a devil's food cake, though firmer in texture. Fluffy chocolate frostings can add extra chocolate impact to cakey brownies. Creaming the butter with the sugar, adding leaveners such as baking powder and baking soda, and slightly reducing the baking time all contribute to a cakey brownie.

On each recipe page is a symbol designating the type of brownie. For brownie dessert recipes such as Cappuccino Frozen Yogurt Brownie Pie or Chocolate-Chocolate Brownie Chunk Cheesecake, the symbol refers to the brownie used in the recipe, rather than the dessert. As you read through our book, you will notice that fudgy brownies are rarely iced, chewy brownies often have nuts, and light, cake-style brownies may feature thick, creamy frostings. Feel free to experiment with your own combinations, but recognize that we have tried to match flavors and textures to yield the best possible brownies. Of course, some brownies may fit into more than one category—perhaps fudgy in the center with chewy edges—and oven temperatures and baking times will also affect the brownies' appearance and texture.

6
TIPS ON BAKING
THE BEST BROWNIES

LINING THE BAKING PAN

To ensure the perfect removal of your brownies from the baking pan, line the bottom and two opposite ends of the pan with overlapping sheets of aluminum foil. Be sure to allow a 2-inch overhang over these ends of the pan. Fold these overhangs down to create "handles." Butter the baking pan, and proceed with your recipe. After the baked brownie is completely cool, run a knife around the sides to release the brownie from the unlined areas. Lift up on the "handles" and remove the entire brownie from the pan. You can now cut the brownie without wasting a crumb.

BAKING BROWNIES

Do not overbake! Overbaked brownies will be dry, crusty, and undesirable. Test your brownies carefully according to the recipe's visual guidelines. *If you want fudgy brownies,* bake only until a wooden toothpick inserted about 1 inch from the side of the pan comes out with a moist crumb. Using this test, the center of the brownie will often seem unbaked, but it will firm upon cooling. To create extra-fudgy brownies, cool the brownie for only 15 minutes, then cover it with aluminum foil and refrigerate. Eat this style of brownie chilled to savor its chocolate fudgelike texture. *For chewy brownies,* bake until a wooden toothpick inserted in the center of the brownie comes out with a moist crumb. *For cakey brownies,* bake until a wooden toothpick inserted in the center of the brownie comes out clean.

STORING BROWNIES

Cool brownies completely before cutting, no matter how tempting a tiny taste may be. This means a minimum of 6 hours at room temperature, and preferably overnight. This allows the flavors to blend and the butter, chocolate, and sugar to set. Blondies are an exception, as we think they taste better warm. If you have used nuts in a brownie recipe, they retain heat, and the brownie will take slightly longer to cool. Cutting nutty brownies before cooling completely will cause the nuts to fall out and the brownies to crumble. We were amazed at the significant overnight changes in the taste and texture of brownies. Surprisingly, most brownies, particularly the fudgy and chewy types, actually improve in flavor after 24 hours (if they last that long)!

Most fudgy brownies will last, uncut, in the pan, covered tightly with plastic wrap and refrigerated, for up to 3 days. Unfrosted brownies may also be cut into squares, wrapped in plastic wrap, and stored in an airtight container at room temperature for up to 3 days. Before wrapping brownies, trim off any undesired dry edges with a serrated knife.

Blondies and peanut-butter brownies are best enjoyed within 24 hours of baking.

7
SPECIAL ADDITIONS

Brownies are often best unadorned, yet special occasions may call for an extra-special touch. The following decorative ideas are suitable for most brownies in this book.

CHOCOLATE CURLS

Use a large chunk of chocolate, such as "break-up" chocolate or premium bulk chocolate, or a 1-ounce square of packaged supermarket chocolate.

1. The chocolate must be at the proper temperature: warm room temperature with low humidity. If the chocolate is too cold, it will splinter and not curl. If your first attempts cause splintering, warm the chocolate by either of these techniques:

   a. Place the chocolate directly under a table lamp for about 5 minutes, until the surface of the chocolate is warm but not melting.

   b. Warm the chocolate in a microwave oven set at medium (50 percent) power for 30 seconds.

   If the chocolate is too warm, it will form soft strips that you may still be able to curl carefully with your fingers.

2. Use a paper towel to hold the chocolate in one hand, so that the heat of your hand doesn't melt the chocolate. Using a swivel-bladed vegetable peeler, make the chocolate curls by pressing down while you "peel" from the upper edge of the smooth side of the chocolate chunk toward you. The harder you press, the thicker

the curls. Let the curls fall onto a wax paper–lined baking sheet, then refrigerate until ready to use.

CHOCOLATE LEAVES

Use firm, clean, nontoxic leaves such as lemon, ivy, galax, or camellia leaves.

1. In the top part of a double boiler over hot, not simmering, water, melt 2 to 4 ounces of high-quality semisweet or bittersweet chocolate, stirring occasionally until smooth. Let cool about 10 minutes, until tepid and slightly thickened.

2. Hold the leaf in the palm of your hand, and using the back of a teaspoon, coat the underside of the leaf evenly and thinly with the melted chocolate. Avoid getting chocolate on the other side of the leaf, or it may break while peeling.

3. Refrigerate the leaves on a wax paper–lined baking sheet for about 15 minutes, until the chocolate is firm. Carefully peel away the leaves from the chocolate, then refrigerate until ready to use.

DECORATIVE CONFECTIONERS' SUGAR AND COCOA PATTERNS

When making decorative patterns from unsweetened cocoa powder, it is best to use alkalized cocoa powder, as its flavor is less harsh than that of the natural, nonalkalized variety.

1. *Patchwork Pattern:* Cut four strips of wax paper, 12″ × 1½″ each. Place the strips diagonally on top of a cooled brownie, leaving a 1½-inch space between the strips. Sift confectioners' sugar or cocoa over the rows of brownie that are exposed between the wax-paper strips. Carefully lift the wax-paper strips, leaving rows of confectioners' sugar or cocoa on the brownie. Repeat the procedure by "crisscrossing" the wax-paper strips in the opposite direction of the confectioners' sugar or cocoa rows. Sift more confectioners' sugar or cocoa over the exposed areas, and remove the wax-paper strips.

2. *Doily Pattern:* Choose a paper doily with a particularly "open" pattern. Place the doily on top of the brownie, and sift confectioners' sugar over the top of the doily

and brownie. Carefully lift the doily, and the decorative lacy sugar pattern will remain.

OTHER DECORATING TIPS

- Hazelnuts, walnuts, pecans, or almonds, half-dipped in chocolate
- Chocolate espresso beans
- Nirvana Brownie Truffles (see Index), rolled into tiny balls and used to decorate frosting and icings

Part II
THE RECIPES

8
BROWNIE CLASSICS

These are our traditional, best-loved brownies—from fudgy to cakey, sometimes studded with toasted walnuts or intense, bittersweet chocolate chunks, more often deep and chocolaty basics—and a couple of golden blondies, of course.

Traditional Fudgy Brownies
Classic Chewy Brownies
Cakey Chocolate Brownies with Cocoa Frosting
Dark Chocolate Iced Brownies
Grandma's Cocoa Brownies
Layered Cheesecake Brownies
Sour Cream Brownies
"The Best-Ever" Triple Chocolate Brownies
Chocolate 'n' Chunk Brownies
Marbled Brownies
Quik-Mix Mint Magic Brownies
Butterscotch Blondies with Chocolate Chunks
Cakey Blondies

 TRADITIONAL FUDGY BROWNIES

The all-American brownie we all know and love. Fudgy, but not wet, sweet, but real chocolaty, with a walnut crunch in every bite. This brownie evokes memories of a blustery wintry day outside, a cozy crackling fire inside, a plateful of fudgy brownies, and a pot of frothy hot chocolate. Yet it is suitable for summertime too—the perfect indulgent ending for a light poolside lunch.

8 tablespoons (1 stick) unsalted butter, cut into pieces
2 ounces unsweetened chocolate, finely chopped
1 cup granulated sugar
2 large eggs, at room temperature

½ teaspoon vanilla extract
½ cup all-purpose flour
⅛ teaspoon salt
2 ounces walnuts, toasted and coarsely chopped (about ½ cup)

1. Position a rack in the center of the oven and preheat to 350°F. Lightly butter and flour an 8-inch square baking pan, tapping out excess flour.

2. In a medium saucepan over low heat, melt butter. Off heat, add chocolate and let stand 1 minute; whisk until smooth. Let stand 10 minutes, until tepid. Whisk in sugar. One at a time, whisk in eggs, then vanilla. Using a wooden spoon, stir in flour and salt. Stir in walnuts.

3. Spread batter evenly into prepared pan and bake 20 to 25 minutes, until a toothpick inserted in the center comes out with a moist crumb. Cool for 15 minutes on a wire cake rack. Cover pan tightly with aluminum foil and refrigerate for at least 4 hours, or overnight.

MAKES 16 BROWNIES

 # CLASSIC CHEWY BROWNIES

One of the best, we think. We have used European bittersweet chocolate for this thick and chewy brownie, as we wanted an intense, rich hit of chocolate that was strong in flavor, yet smooth.

7 tablespoons unsalted butter, cut into pieces
4 ounces European bittersweet chocolate, finely chopped
¾ cup granulated sugar
2 large eggs, at room temperature

1 teaspoon vanilla extract
½ cup all-purpose flour
⅛ teaspoon salt
2 ounces walnuts, toasted and coarsely chopped (about ½ cup)

1. Position a rack in the center of the oven and preheat to 350°F. Lightly butter and flour an 8-inch square baking pan, tapping out excess flour.

2. In a medium saucepan over low heat, melt butter. Off heat, add chocolate and let stand 1 minute; whisk until smooth. Let stand 10 minutes, until tepid. Whisk in sugar. One at a time, whisk in eggs, then vanilla. Using a wooden spoon, stir in flour and salt, just until blended. Stir in walnuts.

3. Spread batter evenly into prepared pan and bake 22 to 27 minutes, until a toothpick inserted in the center comes out with a moist crumb. *Do not overbake.* Cool completely on a wire cake rack.

MAKES 12 BROWNIES

CAKEY CHOCOLATE BROWNIES WITH COCOA FROSTING

When you're craving a lighter brownie with a dark-chocolate taste, try these cake-style brownies with a tender, moist crumb and an old-fashioned cocoa frosting.

BROWNIE

3 ounces semisweet chocolate, coarsely chopped
¼ cup milk
½ teaspoon cider vinegar
¾ cup all-purpose flour
¼ teaspoon baking soda
¼ teaspoon salt
8 tablespoons (1 stick) unsalted butter, at room temperature

¾ cup granulated sugar
2 large eggs, at room temperature
½ teaspoon vanilla extract

FROSTING

4 tablespoons (½ stick) unsalted butter, at room temperature
1 cup confectioners' sugar, sifted
6 tablespoons unsweetened cocoa powder
½ teaspoon vanilla extract
Pinch salt
2 to 3 tablespoons milk

1. *Brownie:* Position a rack in the center of the oven and preheat to 350°F. Lightly butter and flour an 8-inch square baking pan, tapping out excess flour.

2. In the top part of a double boiler, over hot, not simmering, water, melt chocolate. Remove from heat, and cool about 10 minutes, until tepid.

3. In a small bowl, combine milk and vinegar and let stand for 10 minutes, until milk is curdled. Sift flour, baking soda, and salt through a wire strainer onto a sheet of wax paper.

4. In a medium bowl, using a hand-held electric mixer set at high speed, beat butter and sugar for 2 to 3 minutes, until very light in color and texture. One at a time, beat in eggs. Add vanilla and beat for 2 minutes, until the mixture is very light. Beat in melted chocolate. In thirds, alternately beat in flour mixture and milk mixture, scraping the sides of the bowl with a rubber spatula as necessary, just until blended.

5. Spread batter evenly into prepared pan and bake 30 to 35 minutes, until a toothpick inserted in the center comes out clean. Cool completely on a wire cake rack.

6. *Frosting:* In a medium bowl, using a hand-held electric mixer set at low speed, beat butter about 1 minute, until creamy. Gradually beat in confectioners' sugar and cocoa. Beat in vanilla, salt, and enough milk to make the frosting spreadable. Using a metal cake spatula, spread frosting on top of cooled brownie.

MAKES 12 BROWNIES

DARK CHOCOLATE ICED BROWNIES

An old-fashioned chewy brownie with a shiny dark icing, like we used to buy at our favorite hometown bakery—but better, because it's homemade.

BROWNIE

½ cup all-purpose flour
¼ teaspoon baking soda
½ teaspoon salt
3 ounces unsweetened chocolate, finely chopped
4 tablespoons (½ stick) unsalted butter, at room temperature
1 cup packed light brown sugar

2 large eggs, at room temperature
¼ cup sour cream, at room temperature
1 teaspoon vanilla extract

ICING

2 tablespoons unsalted butter
2 ounces unsweetened chocolate, finely chopped
1¾ cups confectioners' sugar, sifted
Pinch salt
1 teaspoon vanilla extract
2 to 3 tablespoons water

1. *Brownie:* Position a rack in the center of the oven and preheat to 350°F. Lightly butter and flour an 8-inch square baking pan. Sift flour, baking soda, and salt through a wire strainer onto a sheet of wax paper.

2. In the top part of a double boiler, over hot, not simmering, water, melt chocolate. Remove from heat, and cool chocolate about 10 minutes, until tepid.

3. In a medium bowl, using a hand-held electric mixer set at high speed, beat butter and brown sugar for 2 to 3 minutes, until light in color and texture. One at a time, add eggs, beating well after each addition. Beat for another minute, until mixture is very thick. Beat in cooled chocolate, sour cream, and vanilla. Beat in flour mixture, just until combined.

4. Spread batter evenly into prepared pan and bake 25 to 30 minutes, until a toothpick inserted in the center comes out clean. Cool completely on a wire cake rack.

5. *Icing:* In a small saucepan over low heat, melt butter. Add chocolate and let stand 1 minute; whisk until smooth. In a small bowl, combine confectioners' sugar and salt. Gradually add chocolate/butter mixture and vanilla; beat in enough water to make spreadable. Spread icing immediately over top of brownie.

MAKES 12 BROWNIES

GRANDMA'S COCOA BROWNIES

Just like Grandma used to make. These chewy brownies have a strong chocolate flavor and a moist crumb, and they make excellent carry-along snacks.

1 cup unsweetened, nonalkalized cocoa powder, such as Hershey's
¾ teaspoon baking soda
½ teaspoon salt
2 teaspoons instant coffee powder
½ cup boiling water
1 cup (2 sticks) unsalted butter, melted

2¼ cups granulated sugar
3 large eggs, at room temperature
1 teaspoon vanilla extract
1½ cups all-purpose flour
4 ounces walnuts, coarsely chopped (about 1 cup) (optional)

1. Position a rack in the center of the oven and preheat to 350°F. Lightly butter and flour a 9″ × 13″ baking pan, tapping out excess flour.

2. Sift cocoa, baking soda, and salt through a wire strainer into a medium bowl. Dissolve coffee powder in boiling water. Whisk coffee liquid and half the melted butter into cocoa mixture until smooth (mixture may look curdled). Whisk in sugar and remaining butter until smooth. One at a time, whisk in eggs, and blend in vanilla. Using a wooden spoon, stir in flour, just until blended. Stir in walnuts, if desired.

3. Spread batter evenly into prepared pan and bake 30 to 35 minutes, until a toothpick inserted in the center comes out with a moist crumb. Cool completely on a wire cake rack.

MAKES 18 TO 24 BROWNIES

LAYERED CHEESECAKE BROWNIES

Best served slightly chilled and eaten with a fork, accompanied by a demitasse of espresso, these brownie squares are sure to impress.

BROWNIE
6 tablespoons (¾ stick) unsalted butter, cut into pieces
3 ounces unsweetened chocolate, finely chopped
1 cup granulated sugar
2 large eggs, at room temperature
1 teaspoon vanilla extract

½ cup all-purpose flour
¼ teaspoon baking soda
¼ teaspoon salt

CHEESECAKE LAYER
1 8-ounce package cream cheese, softened
2 tablespoons unsalted butter, at room temperature
1 large egg, at room temperature
2 tablespoons all-purpose flour
½ teaspoon vanilla extract

1. *Brownie:* Position a rack in the center of the oven and preheat to 350° F. Line an 8-inch square baking pan with aluminum foil so that the foil extends 2 inches over two opposite ends of the pan. Fold the overhang down to form "handles." Butter the bottom of the foil-lined pan.

2. In a medium saucepan, melt butter. Off heat, add chocolate and let stand 1 to 2 minutes; whisk until smooth. Let stand 10 minutes, until tepid. Whisk in sugar. One at a time, whisk in eggs, then vanilla. Using a wooden spoon, stir in flour, baking soda, and salt, just until smooth.

3. Spread batter evenly into prepared pan. Place pan in freezer while preparing cheesecake layer, to help firm the brownie layer.

4. *Cheesecake Layer:* In a medium bowl, using a hand-held electric mixer set at high speed, beat cream cheese and butter for 1 minute, until smooth. Beat in egg, flour, and vanilla.

5. Spread cheesecake layer evenly over top of brownie batter. Bake 30 to 35 minutes, until the edge of the cheesecake layer has risen and set. (The middle will still seem wet but will firm upon standing.) Cool completely on a wire cake rack. These brownies can be stored in the refrigerator, tightly covered with plastic wrap, for up to 3 days.

MAKES 12 BROWNIES

SOUR CREAM BROWNIES

These brownies taste like your favorite devil's food cake, but better. The deep, dark chocolate flavor is heightened with cocoa and accented by a smooth, creamy, sour cream frosting. Positively addictive.

BROWNIE
1¼ cups granulated sugar
½ cup unsweetened, nonalkalized cocoa powder, such as Hershey's
¼ teaspoon baking soda
⅛ teaspoon salt
¼ cup boiling water
8 tablespoons (1 stick) unsalted butter, melted

½ cup all-purpose flour
¼ cup sour cream, at room temperature
1 large egg, at room temperature, lightly beaten
¼ teaspoon vanilla extract

FROSTING
4 ounces semisweet chocolate, finely chopped
¼ cup confectioners' sugar, sifted
⅓ cup sour cream, chilled

1. *Brownie:* Position a rack in the center of the oven and preheat to 350°F. Lightly butter and flour an 8-inch square baking pan, tapping out excess flour.

2. Sift sugar, cocoa, baking soda, and salt into a medium mixing bowl. Whisk in boiling water and melted butter until smooth. Using a wooden spoon, stir in flour, sour cream, egg, and vanilla just until smooth.

3. Spread batter evenly into prepared pan and bake 25 to 30 minutes, until a toothpick inserted in the center comes out with a moist crumb. Cool completely on a wire cake rack.

4. *Frosting:* In the top part of a double boiler, over hot, not simmering, water, melt chocolate. Remove from heat and let stand 10 minutes, until tepid.

5. In a medium bowl, whisk melted chocolate and confectioners' sugar into the sour cream, just until soft peaks form. Do not overbeat. Using a metal cake spatula, spread frosting evenly over the top of the brownie and refrigerate 1 hour, until frosting is set. These brownies can be stored in the refrigerator, tightly covered with plastic wrap, for up to 3 days.

MAKES 16 BROWNIES

"THE BEST-EVER" TRIPLE CHOCOLATE BROWNIES

An explosion of chocolate in every bite, these dynamite brownies are thick with three types of chocolate: unsweetened for strong, bold notes, semisweet for a high roast coffee-like flavor, and European bittersweet for a refined, subtle chocolate profile. A true connoisseur's brownie.

8 tablespoons (1 stick) unsalted butter, cut into pieces

2 ounces unsweetened chocolate, finely chopped

3 ounces bittersweet chocolate, finely chopped

2 large eggs, at room temperature

1 cup packed light brown sugar

2 tablespoons light corn syrup

1 teaspoon vanilla extract

1¼ cups all-purpose flour

¼ teaspoon baking soda

¼ teaspoon salt

1 cup semisweet chocolate chips (1 6-ounce package)

1. Position a rack in the center of the oven and preheat to 350°F. Lightly butter and flour an 8-inch square baking pan, tapping out excess flour.

2. In a medium saucepan over low heat, melt butter. Off heat, add unsweetened and bittersweet chocolate, and let stand 1 minute; whisk until smooth. Let stand until tepid, about 10 minutes.

3. In a medium bowl, using a hand-held electric mixer set at high speed, beat eggs, brown sugar, and corn syrup for 2 minutes, until light in color. Add vanilla, then beat in chocolate mixture, just until blended. Using a wooden spoon, stir in flour, baking soda, and salt, just until blended. Stir in chocolate chips.

4. Spread batter evenly into prepared pan. Bake 28 to 33 minutes, until a toothpick inserted 1 inch from the side of the pan comes out with a moist crumb. Cool completely on a wire cake rack.

MAKES 12 BROWNIES

# CHOCOLATE 'N' CHUNK BROWNIES

Chocolate lovers beware! These dense, rich brownies are studded with semisweet chocolate chunks and spread with a creamy white chocolate frosting.

BROWNIE

½ cup all-purpose flour
¼ teaspoon baking soda
¼ teaspoon salt
6 tablespoons (¾ stick) unsalted butter, cut into pieces
3 ounces unsweetened chocolate, finely chopped

1 cup packed light brown sugar
2 large eggs, at room temperature
1 teaspoon vanilla extract
3 ounces bittersweet or semisweet chocolate, coarsely chopped

FROSTING

3 ounces white chocolate, finely chopped
2 3-ounce packages cream cheese, at cool room temperature
⅓ cup confectioners' sugar

1. *Brownie:* Position a rack in the center of the oven and preheat to 350°F. Lightly butter and flour an 8-inch square baking pan, tapping out excess flour. Sift flour, baking soda, and salt through a wire strainer onto a sheet of wax paper.

2. In a medium saucepan over low heat, melt butter. Off heat, add unsweetened chocolate and let stand 1 to 2 minutes; whisk until smooth. Cool about 10 minutes, until tepid. Whisk in brown sugar. One at a time, whisk in eggs, then vanilla. Using a wooden spoon, stir in flour mixture, just until combined. Stir in chopped chocolate chunks.

3. Spread batter evenly into prepared pan and bake 25 to 30 minutes, until a toothpick inserted in the center comes out with a moist crumb. Cool completely on a wire cake rack.

4. *Frosting:* In the top part of a double boiler, over hot, not simmering, water, melt half the white chocolate, stirring often. (The water should be no warmer than 125°F.) Add remaining white chocolate and melt, stirring often, until smooth. Cool for about 10 minutes, until tepid.

5. In a medium bowl, using a hand-held electric mixer set at high speed, beat cream cheese until smooth. Add cooled white chocolate and confectioners' sugar and beat until light and fluffy. (If the mixture looks curdled, place bowl in freezer for 5 minutes to chill slightly, then rebeat.)

6. Using a metal cake spatula, spread frosting evenly on top of cooled brownie. Refrigerate brownie for 20 minutes to set frosting. These brownies can be stored in the refrigerator, tightly covered with plastic wrap, for up to 3 days.

MAKES 16 BROWNIES

 # MARBLED BROWNIES

Light and dark chocolate batters are swirled together in this attention-getting brownie. Everyone always asks, "How did you do this?" We merely substitute a table knife for an artist's brush.

1 cup all-purpose flour
¼ teaspoon baking soda
¼ teaspoon salt
1 ounce unsweetened chocolate, finely chopped
6 tablespoons (¾ stick) unsalted butter, at room temperature

1 cup granulated sugar
2 large eggs, at room temperature
1 teaspoon vanilla extract

1. Position a rack in the center of the oven and preheat to 350°F. Lightly butter and flour an 8-inch square baking pan, tapping out excess flour. Sift flour, baking soda, and salt onto a sheet of wax paper.

2. In the top part of a double boiler, over hot, not simmering, water, melt chocolate. Remove from heat, and cool about 10 minutes, until tepid.

3. In a medium bowl, using a hand-held electric mixer set at high speed, beat butter and sugar for 2 minutes, until light in color and texture. One at a time, beat in eggs, then vanilla. Using a wooden spoon, stir in flour mixture, just until blended. Divide batter evenly between two bowls. Stir melted chocolate into the batter in one bowl.

4. Place alternating spoonfuls of light and dark batters into prepared pan. Draw a dinner knife through the two batters, swirling them together to get a marbleized effect, and bake 22 to 27 minutes, until a toothpick inserted in the center comes out with a moist crumb. Cool completely on a wire cake rack.

MAKES 12 BROWNIES

QUIK-MIX MINT MAGIC BROWNIES

MMMMmmmmm, mmminty! It's 6:00 P.M. and your in-laws are due for dinner at 7:00 P.M. Chicken with wine and mushrooms is in the oven, but there's no dessert in sight. Grab a box of brownie mix, and in three easy steps, stir up a batch of minty magic. Any mint candy will do, but try chocolate mint wafers or peppermint patties for extra chocolate impact.

MINT BROWNIE
1 23.7-ounce box instant fudge brownie mix
Egg, vegetable oil, and water, according to package directions
2 tablespoons green crème de menthe

ICING
1 cup semisweet chocolate chips (1 6-ounce package)

TOPPING
½ cup crushed hard red-and-white peppermint candies

1. Lightly butter a 9″ × 13″ baking pan. In a large bowl, prepare brownies according to package directions, using crème de menthe in addition to the water called for in the recipe. Spread batter evenly in prepared pan and bake according to package directions.

2. Remove brownie from oven and place on a wire cake rack. Immediately sprinkle top of brownie with chocolate chips. Let stand 5 minutes, until chips are softened. Using a metal cake spatula, spread melted chips evenly over top of brownie.

3. Sprinkle icing with crushed peppermint candies. Refrigerate 10 minutes to set glaze.

MAKES 32 BROWNIES

BUTTERSCOTCH BLONDIES
WITH CHOCOLATE CHUNKS

If you like gooey, barely set blondies, underbake slightly. Our version is chewy on the inside with firm, crusty edges.

8 tablespoons (1 stick) unsalted
    butter, cut into pieces
1 cup packed light brown sugar
1 large egg, lightly beaten
1 teaspoon vanilla extract
1 cup all-purpose flour

1 teaspoon baking powder
¼ teaspoon salt
3 ounces bittersweet or
    semisweet chocolate, coarsely
    chopped

1. Position a rack in the center of the oven and preheat to 350°F. Lightly butter and flour an 8-inch square baking pan, tapping out excess flour.

2. In a medium saucepan over medium heat, melt butter. Add brown sugar and cook for 1 minute, stirring often, until mixture is bubbling. Cool for about 10 minutes, until tepid. Using a wooden spoon, stir in beaten egg and vanilla. Stir in flour, baking powder, and salt, just until combined. Stir in chopped chocolate chunks.

3. Spread batter evenly into prepared pan. Bake 25 to 30 minutes, until a toothpick inserted in the center comes out with a moist crumb. Cool completely on a wire cake rack. (These blondies are also delicious warm.)

MAKES 16 BLONDIES

 # CAKEY BLONDIES

Toasted pecans add a rich, buttery flavor to this cakey golden blondie bar.

8 tablespoons (1 stick) unsalted butter, at room temperature
½ cup packed light brown sugar
¼ cup granulated sugar
2 tablespoons corn syrup
1 large egg, at room temperature

2 teaspoons vanilla extract
1 cup all-purpose flour
1 teaspoon baking powder
¼ teaspoon salt
3 ounces pecans, toasted and coarsely chopped (about ¾ cup)

1. Position a rack in the center of the oven and preheat to 350°F. Lightly butter and flour an 8-inch square baking pan, tapping out excess flour.

2. In a medium bowl, using a hand-held electric mixer set at high speed, beat butter 1 minute, until creamy. Gradually beat in both sugars and corn syrup; continue beating for 2 minutes, until mixture is light in color and texture. Beat in egg, then vanilla. Using a wooden spoon, stir in flour, baking powder, and salt, just until blended. Stir in pecans.

3. Spread batter evenly into prepared pan and bake 23 to 28 minutes, until a toothpick inserted in the center comes out clean. Cool completely on a wire cake rack.

MAKES 12 BLONDIES

9
NUTS ABOUT BROWNIES

The dual texture of a dense, rich, chewy brownie accented by crunchy nuts is a taste pleasure few of us can resist. Peanut butter lovers will go nuts over a double chunky peanut butter brownie with a peanut buttercream frosting. We've also adapted some of our favorite childhood cakes into brownies and created moist, light Banana Walnut Cake Brownies and ultradecadent German Chocolate Brownies

Oatmeal Date-Nut Brownies
Turtle Brownies
German Chocolate Brownies
Coconut Macadamia Brownies
P.B. Peanut Butter Frosted Brownies
Oatmeal Chip 'n' Nut Brownies
Lemon White Brownie Diamonds
Hazelnut Praline Crunch Brownies
Maple-Walnut Iced Brownies
Caramel Peanut Brownies
Budapest Mocha Brownie Bites
Banana Walnut Cake Brownies
Pear and Hazelnut Brownies
Peanut Krispy Brownie Squares

 OATMEAL DATE-NUT BROWNIES

A chewy, moist, chocolate brownie atop a crisp oat-crunch crust is sprinkled with extra oat crunch for a multitextured brownie snack.

OAT-CRUNCH LAYER
2½ cups old-fashioned rolled
  oats (*not* quick-cooking oats)
¾ cup all-purpose flour
¾ cup packed light brown sugar
½ teaspoon baking soda
12 tablespoons (1½ sticks)
  unsalted butter, melted

DATE BROWNIE
10 tablespoons (1 stick plus 2
  tablespoons) unsalted butter,
  cut into pieces
4 ounces unsweetened
  chocolate, finely chopped
2 cups granulated sugar
4 large eggs, at room
  temperature

1 teaspoon vanilla extract
1¼ cups all-purpose flour
1 teaspoon baking powder
1 teaspoon salt
1 8-ounce package chopped
  dates
2 ounces walnuts, coarsely
  chopped (about ½ cup)

1. *Oat-Crunch Layer:* Position a rack in the center of the oven and preheat to 350°F. Lightly butter a 9″ × 13″ baking pan.

2. In a medium bowl, combine oats, flour, brown sugar, and baking soda; stir in melted butter. Set aside ¾ cup of oat mixture. Press remaining oat mixture into bottom of prepared pan. Bake 10 minutes, just until set, and cool slightly.

3. *Date Brownie:* In a medium saucepan over low heat, melt butter. Off heat, add chocolate. Let stand 1 minute; whisk until smooth. Let stand 10 minutes, until tepid. Whisk in sugar. One at a time, add eggs, whisking well after each addition, then whisk in vanilla. Using a wooden spoon, stir in flour, baking powder, and salt, just until blended.

4. Sprinkle dates and walnuts evenly over oat-crunch layer. Spread brownie batter evenly over oat layer. Sprinkle reserved oat mixture on top of brownie batter and bake about 30 minutes, until a toothpick inserted in the center comes out with a moist crumb. Cool completely on a wire cake rack.

MAKES 28 BROWNIES

# TURTLE BROWNIES

Chewy, buttery caramel sprinkled with toasted pecans, sandwiched between moist, rich, chocolaty brownie layers.

CARAMEL LAYER

2 14-ounce packages caramels, unwrapped
1 12-ounce can evaporated milk

2 ounces pecans, toasted and coarsely chopped (about ½ cup)

BROWNIE LAYERS

11 tablespoons (1 stick plus 3 tablespoons) unsalted butter, cut into pieces
4 ounces unsweetened chocolate, finely chopped
2 cups packed light brown sugar
4 large eggs, at room temperature
1 teaspoon vanilla extract
1¼ cups all-purpose flour
1 teaspoon baking powder
½ teaspoon salt

1. *Caramel Layer:* In a heavy-bottomed medium saucepan, melt caramels and evaporated milk over low heat, stirring constantly, for 5 to 8 minutes, until smooth. Remove from heat and keep warm.

2. *Brownie Layers:* Position a rack in the center of the oven and preheat to 350°F. Line a 9″ × 13″ baking pan with a double thickness of aluminum foil so that the foil extends 2 inches beyond the two short ends of the pan. Fold the overhang down to form "handles." Butter the bottom and sides of the foil-lined pan.

3. In a medium saucepan over low heat, melt butter. Off heat, add chocolate and let stand 1 minute; whisk until smooth. Let stand 10 minutes, until tepid. Whisk in brown sugar. One at a time, whisk in eggs, then vanilla. Using a wooden spoon, stir in flour, baking powder, and salt.

4. Spread half of the batter evenly into the prepared pan. Bake 12 to 15 minutes only, just until top is set. Using a lightly oiled metal cake spatula, spread warm caramel evenly over top of brownie layer. Sprinkle pecans over caramel layer. Spread remaining brownie batter evenly over top of caramel. Bake for an additional 12 to 15 minutes, just until a toothpick inserted into the top brownie layer (but not the caramel) comes out clean. Cool completely on a wire cake rack. Run a knife around the inside edges of the pan to release the brownie from the sides. Lift up on "handles" to remove brownie. Using a sharp, oiled knife, cut into 32 bars.

MAKES 32 BROWNIES

 # GERMAN CHOCOLATE BROWNIES

This is Joan's favorite childhood birthday cake baked into a moist, cakelike brownie form with the thick and sweet traditional coconut-pecan frosting.

BROWNIE
4 ounces sweet chocolate (such as Baker's German's), finely chopped
8 tablespoons (1 stick) unsalted butter, at room temperature
⅔ cup granulated sugar
2 large eggs, at room temperature
1 teaspoon vanilla extract
¾ cup all-purpose flour
⅛ teaspoon salt

FROSTING
½ cup sweetened condensed milk
4 tablespoons (½ stick) unsalted butter
2 large egg yolks
¾ cup sweetened coconut flakes
2 ounces pecans, coarsely chopped (about ½ cup)
½ teaspoon vanilla extract

1. *Brownie:* Position a rack in the center of the oven and preheat to 350°F. Lightly butter and flour an 8-inch square baking pan, tapping out excess flour.

2. In the top part of a double boiler, over hot, not simmering, water, melt chocolate. Remove from heat, and let stand about 10 minutes, until tepid.

3. In a medium bowl, using a hand-held electric mixer set at high speed, beat butter and sugar for 2 to 3 minutes, until light in color and texture. One at a time, beat in eggs, then vanilla. Reduce the mixer speed to low and beat in flour and salt, scraping the sides of the bowl with a rubber spatula.

4. Spread batter evenly into prepared pan and bake 25 to 30 minutes, until a toothpick inserted in the center comes out with a moist crumb. *Do not overbake.* Cool completely on a wire cake rack.

5. *Frosting:* In a medium saucepan over medium-low heat, combine condensed milk, butter, and egg yolks and simmer, stirring constantly, for about 4 minutes, until thickened. Transfer mixture to a medium bowl and stir in coconut, pecans, and vanilla. Cool, stirring occasionally, about 5 minutes, until thick enough to spread. Spread frosting over top of cooled brownie. Refrigerate about 30 minutes, until frosting is firm. Store in the refrigerator, tightly covered with plastic wrap, until ready to serve. Remove from refrigerator 30 minutes before serving.

MAKES 12 BROWNIES

# COCONUT MACADAMIA BROWNIES

The moistness of flaked coconut in a rich cocoa batter and the crunch of toasted macadamia nuts sprinkled on top provide a mélange of flavors and textures in this unusual chewy brownie.

½ cup all-purpose flour
½ cup unsweetened alkalized cocoa powder, such as Droste
¼ teaspoon baking powder
¼ teaspoon salt
¾ cup plus 2 tablespoons granulated sugar
2 large eggs, at room temperature

1 teaspoon vanilla extract
16 tablespoons (2 sticks) unsalted butter, melted
¾ cup sweetened coconut flakes
2 ounces macadamia nuts, rinsed of salt, patted dry, and coarsely chopped (about ½ cup)

1. Position a rack in the center of the oven and preheat to 350°F. Lightly butter and flour an 8-inch square baking pan, tapping out excess flour. Sift flour, cocoa, baking powder, and salt through a wire strainer onto a sheet of wax paper.

2. In a medium bowl, using a hand-held electric mixer set at high speed, beat sugar, eggs, and vanilla for 1 to 2 minutes, until thickened and very light in color. Using a wooden spoon, stir in cocoa mixture and melted butter, just until smooth. Stir in coconut.

3. Spread batter evenly into prepared pan. Sprinkle chopped macadamia nuts evenly over top of brownie. Bake 28 to 33 minutes, until a toothpick inserted in the center comes out with a moist crumb. Cool completely on a wire cake rack.

MAKES 12 BROWNIES

# P.B. PEANUT BUTTER FROSTED BROWNIES

Peanut butter is definitely our second favorite flavor, and this fluffy, frosted, all–peanut-butter brownie packs a pretty powerful peanutty punch.

BROWNIE	PEANUT BUTTERCREAM
⅓ cup chunky peanut butter	¼ cup chunky peanut butter
3 tablespoons unsalted butter, at room temperature	2 tablespoons unsalted butter, at room temperature
1 cup packed light brown sugar	1 cup confectioners' sugar, sifted
2 large eggs, at room temperature	1 tablespoon milk
1 teaspoon vanilla extract	½ teaspoon vanilla extract
¾ cup all-purpose flour	2 ounces salted peanuts (not dry-roasted), rinsed of salt, patted dry, and coarsely chopped (about ½ cup)
1 teaspoon baking powder	
½ teaspoon salt	
½ cup peanut butter chips	

1. *Brownie:* Position a rack in the center of the oven and preheat to 350°F. Lightly butter a 9-inch square baking pan.

2. In a medium bowl, using a hand-held electric mixer set at high speed, beat peanut butter and butter about 1 minute, until well combined. Add brown sugar and beat 2 to 3 minutes, until very light in color. One at a time, beat in eggs, then add vanilla. Using a wooden spoon, stir in flour, baking powder, and salt, just until blended. Stir in peanut butter chips.

3. Spread batter into prepared pan and bake 25 to 30 minutes, until a toothpick inserted in the center comes out clean. Cool completely on a wire cake rack.

4. *Peanut Buttercream:* In a medium bowl, using a hand-held electric mixer set at high speed, beat peanut butter and butter until well combined. Gradually beat in confectioners' sugar. Beat in milk and vanilla. Spread frosting evenly over top of cooled brownie and sprinkle evenly with peanuts. Cover brownie with plastic wrap and refrigerate 1 hour, until frosting is firm.

MAKES 9 EXTRA-LARGE BROWNIES

OATMEAL CHIP 'N' NUT BROWNIES

An old-fashioned brownie with an almost gooey center and a chocolaty-chip walnut crunch in every bite. Blondie lovers will especially enjoy the familiar butterscotch flavor and chewy texture.

⅔ cup old-fashioned rolled oats (*not* quick-cooking oats), divided
8 tablespoons (1 stick) unsalted butter, softened
½ cup granulated sugar
½ cup packed light brown sugar
2 large eggs, at room temperature

½ teaspoon vanilla extract
½ cup all-purpose flour
¼ teaspoon baking powder
½ teaspoon salt
6 ounces semisweet chocolate chips (about 1 cup)
3 ounces walnuts, coarsely chopped (about ¾ cup)

1. Position a rack in the center of the oven and preheat to 350°F. Lightly butter an 8-inch square baking pan.

2. In a blender or a food processor fitted with the metal blade, process ⅓ cup of the oats until finely ground into a "flour." In a medium bowl, using a hand-held electric mixer set at high speed, beat the butter for 1 minute, until creamy. Add both sugars and beat about 1 minute, until light in color. One at a time, beat in eggs, then vanilla. Using a wooden spoon, stir in flour, ground oats, remaining $\frac{1}{3}$ cup oats, baking powder, and salt. Stir in chocolate chips and walnuts.

3. Spread batter evenly into prepared pan and bake 25 to 30 minutes, until a toothpick inserted in the center comes out with a moist crumb. Cool completely on a wire cake rack.

MAKES 16 BROWNIES

LEMON WHITE BROWNIE DIAMONDS

The refreshingly tart lemon flavor balances the sweetness of the white chocolate in these thick, cake-style brownie jewels with an almond-crisp crust.

ALMOND-CRISP CRUST

4 ounces (about 1 cup) slivered almonds, toasted (see Index)
2 tablespoons light brown sugar
2 tablespoons unsalted butter, at room temperature

LEMON WHITE CHOCOLATE BROWNIE

6 tablespoons (¾ stick) unsalted butter, cut into pieces
3 ounces white chocolate, finely chopped
2 large eggs, at room temperature
½ cup packed light brown sugar
½ cup granulated sugar
Grated zest of 1 medium lemon
½ teaspoon vanilla extract
¼ teaspoon almond extract
1¼ cups all-purpose flour
½ teaspoon baking powder
¼ teaspoon salt
1 ounce sliced almonds (about ¼ cup)

1. *Almond-Crisp Crust:* Position a rack in the center of the oven and preheat to 350°F. Lightly butter and flour an 8-inch square baking pan, tapping out excess flour.

2. In a blender or a food processor fitted with the metal blade, pulse almonds until finely chopped. In a small bowl, work chopped almonds, brown sugar, and butter between your fingers until well mixed. Press the mixture evenly in the bottom of the prepared pan.

3. *Brownie:* In a medium saucepan, melt butter over low heat. Off heat, add half of the white chocolate and let stand 30 seconds. Whisk until almost smooth. Add remaining white chocolate and let stand 1 minute; whisk until smooth. Let stand about 10 minutes, until tepid.

4. In a medium bowl, using a hand-held electric mixer set at high speed, beat eggs and both sugars for 2 to 3 minutes, until thick and light in color. Beat in cooled white chocolate, lemon zest, and both extracts. Using a wooden spoon, stir in flour, baking powder, and salt.

5. Spread batter evenly over crust. Sprinkle top of batter with sliced almonds, patting almonds down slightly onto batter. Bake 30 to 35 minutes, until a toothpick inserted in the center comes out with a moist crumb. Cool completely on a wire cake rack. Cut brownies into nine squares; cut each square diagonally to make 18 triangles.

MAKES 18 TRIANGLES

HAZELNUT PRALINE CRUNCH BROWNIES

A sophisticated variation that features a caramelized hazelnut crunch in a dense, thick, chocolate brownie. Do not attempt to make praline on a humid or rainy day.

PRALINE
¼ cup granulated sugar
2 tablespoons water
Few drops lemon juice
4 ounces (about 1 cup) hazelnuts, toasted and skinned (see Index)

BROWNIE
½ cup plus 2 tablespoons all-purpose flour
¼ teaspoon baking soda
¼ teaspoon salt
7 tablespoons unsalted butter, cut into pieces
4 ounces bittersweet chocolate, finely chopped
⅔ cup packed light brown sugar
2 large eggs, at room temperature
2 tablespoons hazelnut-flavored liqueur, such as Frangelico
1 teaspoon vanilla extract

GLAZE
¼ cup heavy cream
4 ounces bittersweet or semisweet chocolate, finely chopped

1. *Praline:* Lightly oil a baking sheet. In a heavy-bottomed small saucepan, over medium heat, stir together sugar, water, and lemon juice until the mixture comes to a boil. Stop stirring, and cook 3 to 4 minutes, washing down any sugar crystals that form on the sides of the pan with a wet pastry brush, until syrup is light amber-brown. Stir in hazelnuts. Pour mixture out onto the prepared baking sheet and let stand at room temperature for at least 1 hour, until hard. Using a sharp knife, coarsely chop praline. Praline can be made up to 2 weeks ahead, covered tightly, and stored at room temperature

2. *Brownie:* Position a rack in the center of the oven and preheat to 350°F. Lightly butter an 8-inch square baking pan. Sift flour, baking soda, and salt through a wire strainer onto a sheet of wax paper.

3. In a medium saucepan over low heat, melt butter. Off heat, add chocolate and let stand 1 minute; whisk until smooth. Let stand 10 minutes, until tepid. Whisk in brown sugar. One at a time, whisk in eggs, liqueur, then vanilla. Using a wooden spoon, stir in flour mixture, just until blended. Stir in ¾ cup of the chopped praline.

4. Spread batter evenly into prepared pan and bake 22 to 27 minutes, until a toothpick inserted in the center comes out with a moist crumb. Cool completely on a wire cake rack.

5. *Glaze:* In a small saucepan over low heat, bring cream to a simmer. Off heat, add chocolate and let stand 1 minute; whisk until smooth. Let stand 15 minutes, until tepid and slightly thickened. Using a metal cake spatula, spread glaze evenly over top of brownie. Sprinkle glaze evenly with remaining chopped praline. Refrigerate 20 minutes only, to set glaze. Do not store brownie in the refrigerator, or the praline will melt. Using a serrated knife, cut brownie into 12 squares.

MAKES 12 BROWNIES

MAPLE-WALNUT ICED BROWNIES

These chewy, nutty brownies evoke memories of a crisp autumn afternoon. We enjoy them with a mug of hot mulled apple cider.

BROWNIE
3 ounces semisweet chocolate, finely chopped
1 cup all-purpose flour
⅓ cup packed light brown sugar
1 teaspoon baking powder
¼ teaspoon salt
¼ cup maple syrup

4 tablespoons (½ stick) unsalted butter, melted
1 large egg, lightly beaten, at room temperature
2 ounces walnuts, coarsely chopped (about ½ cup)

ICING
¾ cup confectioners' sugar, sifted
1 tablespoon milk
½ teaspoon maple extract
12 large walnut halves, for garnish

1. *Brownie:* Position a rack in the center of the oven and preheat to 350°F. Lightly butter and flour an 8-inch square baking pan, tapping out excess flour.

2. In the top part of a double boiler, over hot, not simmering, water, melt chocolate. Remove from heat and let stand about 10 minutes, until tepid.

3. In a medium bowl, mix together flour, brown sugar, baking powder, and salt. Add maple syrup, melted butter, and egg, and stir just until blended. Stir in cooled chocolate. Stir in walnuts.

4. Spread batter evenly into prepared pan and bake 22 to 28 minutes, until a toothpick inserted in the center comes out with a moist crumb. Cool completely on a wire cake rack.

5. *Icing:* In a medium bowl, whisk together confectioners' sugar, milk, and maple extract until smooth. Using a metal cake spatula, spread icing evenly over top of brownie. Cut into 12 squares, placing a walnut half in the center of each brownie.

MAKES 12 BROWNIES

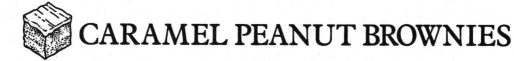

CARAMEL PEANUT BROWNIES

The fulfilling crunch of roasted peanuts, the toothsome tug of chewy, buttery caramel, and, of course, a thick chocolate fudge brownie. Satisfaction guaranteed.

BROWNIE
8 tablespoons (1 stick) unsalted butter, cut into pieces
4 ounces semisweet chocolate, finely chopped
¾ cup packed light brown sugar
2 large eggs, at room temperature
1 teaspoon vanilla extract
½ cup all-purpose flour
⅛ teaspoon baking powder
¼ teaspoon salt

CARAMEL PEANUT TOPPING
1 14-ounce package caramels, unwrapped
3 tablespoons milk
4 ounces salted peanuts (not dry-roasted), rinsed of salt, patted dry, and coarsely chopped (about ½ cup)

1. *Brownie:* Position a rack in the center of the oven and preheat to 350°F. Line an 8-inch square baking pan with a double thickness of aluminum foil so that the foil extends 2 inches over two opposite ends of the pan. Fold the overhang down to form "handles." Butter the bottom and sides of the foil-lined pan.

2. In a medium saucepan over low heat, melt butter. Off heat, add chocolate and let stand 1 minute; whisk until smooth. Let stand 10 minutes, until tepid. Whisk in sugar. Whisk in eggs, one at a time, then vanilla. Using a wooden spoon, stir in flour, baking powder, and salt.

3. Spread batter evenly into prepared pan and bake 20 to 25 minutes, until a toothpick inserted in the center comes out with a moist crumb. Cool completely on a wire cake rack.

4. *Topping:* In a heavy-bottomed medium saucepan over low heat, melt caramels and milk, stirring constantly, for 4 to 7 minutes, until smooth. Let stand 10 minutes, until slightly cooled. Using a lightly oiled metal cake spatula, spread caramel topping evenly over brownie and sprinkle evenly with peanuts. Let stand 1 hour at room temperature to set topping. Run a knife around inside edges of pan to release brownie from sides. Lift up on the "handles" to remove brownie. Using a lightly oiled sharp knife, cut into 16 squares.

MAKES 16 BROWNIES

BUDAPEST MOCHA BROWNIE BITES

The espresso of the brownie world, these sophisticated miniature brownies are bittersweet, intensely chocolate, and have a strong coffee flavor. As in a mocha-walnut Hungarian Ilona torte, very finely chopped walnuts are substituted for some of the flour.

BROWNIE
8 tablespoons (1 stick) unsalted
   butter, cut into pieces
3 ounces unsweetened
   chocolate, finely chopped
½ teaspoon espresso coffee
   powder dissolved in
   1 tablespoon boiling water
2 large eggs, at room
   temperature

1 cup packed light brown sugar
1 teaspoon vanilla extract
⅓ cup all-purpose flour
1 ounce walnuts, very finely
   chopped (about ¼ cup)
¼ teaspoon salt

GLAZE
¼ cup heavy cream
4 ounces semisweet chocolate,
   finely chopped
¼ teaspoon instant espresso
   powder dissolved in
   2 teaspoons boiling water
24 chocolate espresso beans, for
   garnish

1. *Brownie:* Position a rack in the center of the oven and preheat to 350°F. Line the bottom of an 8-inch square baking pan with aluminum foil and lightly butter the foil.

2. In a medium saucepan over low heat, melt butter. Off heat, add chocolate and dissolved espresso and let stand 1 minute; whisk until smooth. Let stand 10 minutes, until tepid.

3. In a medium bowl, using a hand-held electric mixer set at high speed, beat eggs and brown sugar for 2 minutes, until light in texture and color. Beat in chocolate mixture, then vanilla. Using a wooden spoon, stir in flour, walnuts, and salt.

4. Spread batter evenly into prepared pan and bake 20 to 25 minutes, until a toothpick inserted in the center comes out with a moist crumb. Cool completely on a wire cake rack. Run a knife around the inside edges of the pan to release brownie from sides. Invert brownie onto the wire cake rack, remove pan, and carefully peel off foil.

5. *Glaze:* In a medium saucepan over low heat, bring cream to a low simmer. Off heat, add chocolate and dissolved espresso mixture and let stand 1 minute; whisk until smooth. Let stand 15 minutes, until cooled and slightly thickened. Using a metal cake spatula, spread glaze evenly over top of brownie. Refrigerate 30 minutes to set glaze. Using a hot, wet knife, cut brownie into 24 squares and top each with a chocolate espresso bean.

MAKES 24 BROWNIES

BANANA WALNUT CAKE BROWNIES

A light cake-style brownie based on our favorite breakfast fruit bread—wonderful warm from the oven for an early morning treat with a cup of frothy hot chocolate, or served with a dollop of walnut-dusted whipped cream as an indulgent dessert.

BROWNIE
6 tablespoons (¾ stick) unsalted butter, cut into pieces
2 tablespoons vegetable oil
2 ounces unsweetened chocolate, finely chopped
½ cup granulated sugar
½ cup packed light brown sugar
2 large eggs, at room temperature
½ teaspoon vanilla extract
1 cup all-purpose flour
¾ cup mashed ripe bananas (about 2 medium)
1 teaspoon baking powder
½ teaspoon salt
2 ounces walnuts, toasted and coarsely chopped (about ½ cup)

GARNISH
2 ounces semisweet or bittersweet chocolate
1 teaspoon solid vegetable shortening, such as Crisco
12 large walnut halves

1. *Brownie:* Position a rack in the center of the oven and preheat to 350°F. Lightly butter and flour an 8-inch square baking pan, tapping out excess flour.

2. In a medium saucepan over low heat, melt butter with vegetable oil. Off heat, add chocolate and let stand 1 minute; whisk until smooth. Let stand 10 minutes, until tepid. Whisk in both sugars. One at a time, whisk in eggs, then vanilla. Using a wooden spoon, stir in flour, mashed bananas, baking powder, and salt, just until blended. Stir in chopped walnuts.

3. Spread batter evenly into prepared pan, and bake 25 to 30 minutes, until a toothpick inserted 1 inch from the edge of the brownie comes out clean. Cool completely on a wire cake rack.

4. *Garnish:* In a double boiler, over hot, not simmering, water, melt chocolate and shortening, stirring often, until smooth. Remove from heat; let stand 10 minutes, until slightly thickened and tepid. Transfer to a small custard cup or bowl. One at a time, dip half of each walnut in chocolate. Scrape bottom of walnut on edge of custard cup to remove excess chocolate, and place on a wax paper–lined baking sheet. Refrigerate for 10 minutes, or until chocolate is firm. Cut brownie into 12 squares, and place a walnut half on each square.

MAKES 12 BROWNIES

PEAR AND HAZELNUT BROWNIES

The memorable combination of pear and chocolate, known to most dessert lovers as "Pears Hélène," provides the basis for this Continental brownie creation. We've added toasted hazelnuts and a chocolate-hazelnut icing.

PEAR PUREE
3 medium pears, peeled, cored, and coarsely chopped
¼ cup granulated sugar
1 teaspoon lemon juice

BROWNIE
8 tablespoons (1 stick) unsalted butter, cut into pieces
2 ounces unsweetened chocolate, finely chopped
1 cup packed light brown sugar
1 large egg, at room temperature
1 cup all-purpose flour

1 teaspoon baking powder
¼ teaspoon salt
2 ounces hazelnuts, skinned, toasted, and coarsely chopped (about ½ cup) (see Index)

½ cup Nutella (chocolate-hazelnut spread)

1. *Pear Puree:* In a small saucepan, combine pears, sugar, and lemon juice, and cook, covered, over low heat for 5 minutes, until pears are tender. Increase heat to medium and cook, uncovered, for 8 to 10 minutes, stirring often and mashing pears with a wooden spoon, until liquid is evaporated and mixture forms a coarse puree. Cool completely.

2. *Brownie:* Position a rack in the center of the oven and preheat to 350°F. Lightly butter and flour a 9-inch square baking pan, tapping out excess flour.

3. In a medium saucepan over low heat, melt butter. Off heat, add chocolate and let stand 1 minute; whisk until smooth. Cool until tepid, about 10 minutes. Stir in brown sugar. Stir in egg. Add flour, pear puree, baking powder, and salt, and stir just until smooth. Stir in coarsely chopped hazelnuts.

4. Spread batter evenly into prepared pan and bake 25 to 30 minutes, until a toothpick inserted in the center comes out with a moist crumb. Cool completely on a wire cake rack. Spread Nutella evenly over top of cooled brownie. Refrigerate for 30 minutes to set Nutella.

MAKES 12 BROWNIES

# PEANUT KRISPY BROWNIE SQUARES

Just imagine a thick hunk of chocolaty cakelike brownie dotted with peanuts, then consider a crispy, crunchy topping enhanced with peanut butter flavor. Satisfied yet?

BROWNIE
6 tablespoons (¾ stick) unsalted butter, cut into pieces
2 ounces unsweetened chocolate, finely chopped
1 cup packed light brown sugar
2 large eggs, at room temperature
½ teaspoon vanilla extract

½ cup plus 2 tablespoons all-purpose flour
½ teaspoon baking soda
½ teaspoon salt
2 ounces salted peanuts (not dry-roasted), rinsed of salt and patted dry (about ½ cup)

TOPPING
1 cup peanut butter chips
1 teaspoon solid vegetable shortening, such as Crisco
1 cup crispy rice cereal

1. *Brownie:* Position a rack in the center of the oven and preheat to 350°F. Lightly butter and flour a 9-inch square baking pan, tapping out excess flour.

2. In a medium saucepan over low heat, melt butter. Off heat, add chocolate and let stand 1 minute; whisk until smooth. Let stand 10 minutes, until tepid. Whisk in brown sugar. One at a time, whisk in eggs, then vanilla. Using a wooden spoon, stir in flour, baking soda, and salt, just until blended. Stir in peanuts.

3. Spread batter evenly into prepared pan and bake 18 to 24 minutes, until a toothpick inserted in the center comes out with a moist crumb. Cool completely on a wire cake rack.

4. *Topping:* In the top part of a double boiler, over hot, not simmering, water, melt peanut butter chips and shortening, stirring often, until smooth. Stir in rice cereal. Remove from heat, and using a metal cake spatula, spread topping evenly over brownie. Refrigerate for 30 minutes to set topping. Using a serrated knife, carefully "saw" through the topping, then cut down to form 16 squares.

MAKES 16 BROWNIES

10
SOMETHING BORROWED, SOMETHING NEW

Over the years we have shared many memorable experiences with dear friends who share our passion for baking. The first half of this chapter is a tribute to these close friends and fellow foodies, whose recipe secrets we pass along to you. We have also developed a collection of novel recipes, from a tender, light Brownie Muffin to a visually striking Patchwork Brownie adorned with crisscrossing stripes of cocoa and powdered sugar.

SOMETHING BORROWED

Michael's Aztec Brownies
Irena's Hollywood Brownies
Rose's Best Bittersweet Brownies
Richard's Coconut Blondies
Adrienne's Incredible Microwave Brownies
Flo's White Chocolate Raspberry Brownie Petits Fours
Barb's Fudgy Food-Processor Brownies
Beth's Amaretti Truffle Brownies
Beverly's Chewies

SOMETHING NEW

Brownie Muffins
Gingered Applesauce Brownie Squares
Raspberry Truffled Brownies
Patchwork Brownies
Rainbow Brownies
St. Valentine's Strawberry Brownie Hearts
Minty Cream Chip Brownies
Prune-Armagnac Brownies
Peanut-Butter-and-Jelly Bars
Granola Brownie Squares
White-on-White Fantasy Brownies
Cranberry Holiday Brownie Fudge
Coffee-and-Cream Brownies
Candy Bar Brownies
Campsite Raisin Brownies
Zebra Brownies
Tropical Paradise Brownies
S'more Brownies

MICHAEL'S AZTEC BROWNIES

Southwestern cuisine is HOT, HOT, HOT, and Michael McLaughlin, cookbook author and chili expert, has shared with us his favorite Tex-Mex brownie with a bite. Chilling the brownies overnight enhances the fudgy texture.

12 tablespoons (1½ sticks) unsalted butter, cut into pieces
4 ounces unsweetened chocolate, finely chopped
1 teaspoon instant espresso powder dissolved in 1 tablespoon boiling water
½ teaspoon ground cinnamon
¼ teaspoon black pepper
¼ teaspoon cayenne pepper
3 large eggs, at room temperature
1½ cups packed light brown sugar
2 teaspoons vanilla extract
¼ teaspoon salt
1 cup all-purpose flour
4 ounces walnuts, coarsely chopped (about 1 cup)

1. Position a rack in the center of the oven and preheat to 350°F. Line the bottom of an 8-inch square baking pan with aluminum foil, and lightly butter the bottom and sides of the foil-lined pan.

2. In a medium saucepan over low heat, melt butter. Off heat, add chocolate, coffee liquid, cinnamon, and both peppers. Let stand 1 minute; whisk until smooth. Let stand 10 minutes, until tepid.

3. In a medium bowl, whisk eggs until foamy. Add sugar and whisk 1 minute, until thickened. Beat in vanilla and salt. Using a rubber spatula, fold in chocolate mixture. Fold in flour, just until blended. Stir in walnuts.

4. Spread batter evenly into prepared pan. Bake 22 to 25 minutes, until brownie appears dry around the edges but a toothpick inserted 1 inch from the edge comes out with a very moist crumb. (The center will appear very moist.) Cool completely on a wire cake rack. Cover pan with aluminum foil and refrigerate at least 6 hours, or overnight.

5. Run a knife around inside edge of pan to release brownie from sides. Place a cutting board on top of brownie pan, invert, remove pan, and carefully peel off foil. Bring brownies to room temperature before serving.

MAKES 16 BROWNIES

IRENA'S HOLLYWOOD BROWNIES

Irena Chalmers, prolific cookbook author, says that these brownies are called "Hollywood Brownies" because they are always the stars of her dessert table.

11 tablespoons (1 stick plus
   3 tablespoons) unsalted
   butter, cut into pieces
5 ounces unsweetened
   chocolate, finely chopped
4 large eggs, at room
   temperature
1 cup granulated sugar

1 cup packed light brown sugar
2 teaspoons vanilla extract
2 cups sifted all-purpose flour
2 teaspoons baking powder
1 teaspoon salt
4 ounces walnuts or pecans,
   coarsely chopped (about
   1 cup) (optional)

1. Position a rack in the center of the oven and preheat to 350°F. Lightly butter a 9-inch square baking pan.

2. In a medium saucepan over low heat, melt butter. Off heat, add chocolate and let stand 1 minute; whisk until smooth. Cool 10 minutes, until tepid.

3. In a medium bowl, using a hand-held electric mixer set at high speed, beat eggs for 2 to 3 minutes, until pale yellow and thickened. Add both sugars and vanilla and beat until well combined. Beat in melted chocolate. Add flour, baking powder, and salt, and beat just until combined. Using a wooden spoon, stir in nuts, if desired.

4. Spread batter evenly into prepared pan and bake 35 to 45 minutes, until a toothpick inserted in the center comes out clean. Cool completely on a wire cake rack.

MAKES 16 BROWNIES

ROSE'S BEST BITTERSWEET BROWNIES

Rose Levy Beranbaum, cookbook author and baking authority, prefers her brownies "pure, moist, and intensely bittersweet." Chopped pecans add rich buttery flavor to this deep, dark chocolate brownie.

4 ounces European bittersweet chocolate, finely chopped
8 tablespoons (1 stick) unsalted butter, cut into pieces
½ cup granulated sugar
2 large eggs, at room temperature
½ teaspoon vanilla extract
¼ cup all-purpose flour
Pinch salt
2 ounces pecans, coarsely chopped (about ½ cup)

1. Position a rack in the center of the oven and preheat to 350°F. Line the bottom of an 8-inch square baking pan with wax paper. Lightly butter and flour the inside of the pan, tapping out excess flour.

2. In the top part of a double boiler, over hot, not simmering, water, melt chocolate and butter, stirring often, until smooth. Remove from heat and let stand 10 minutes, until tepid. Whisk in sugar. One at a time, whisk in eggs, then vanilla. Using a wooden spoon, stir in flour and salt, just until blended. Stir in pecans.

3. Spread batter evenly into prepared pan and bake 20 to 25 minutes, until a toothpick inserted 1 inch from the side of the pan comes out with a moist crumb. (The center will appear quite wet.) Cool for 20 minutes on a wire cake rack. Run a knife around the inside edge of the pan to release brownie from sides, and invert brownie onto a lightly buttered baking sheet. Carefully peel off wax paper, invert again onto a wire cake rack, and cool completely. Using a sharp knife, cut into 16 squares. Wrap each brownie tightly in plastic wrap.

MAKES 16 BROWNIES

 # RICHARD'S COCONUT BLONDIES

The combination of chocolate and coconut, which has made many Mounds Bar fans, is here transformed by Richard Sax into a chewy bar cookie, generously studded with semisweet chocolate chips, moist coconut, and buttery pecans. Richard is the author of several cookbooks and contributes regularly to many national publications, including a monthly column in Bon Appétit. *P.S. He loves chocolate desserts too.*

1 cup plus 2 tablespoons
   all-purpose flour
½ teaspoon baking soda
¼ teaspoon salt
8 tablespoons (1 stick) unsalted
   butter, at room temperature
⅓ cup granulated sugar
⅓ cup packed light brown sugar
1 large egg, at room
   temperature

1 teaspoon vanilla extract
1 cup semisweet chocolate chips
   (1 6-ounce package)
1¼ cups sweetened coconut
   flakes
2 ounces pecans, toasted and
   coarsely chopped (about
   ½ cup)

1. Position a rack in the center of the oven and preheat to 350°F. Lightly butter a 9-inch square baking pan.

2. Sift flour, baking soda, and salt through a fine wire strainer onto a sheet of wax paper. In a medium bowl, using a hand-held electric mixer set at high speed, cream butter and sugars for 2 minutes, until very light in color and texture. Beat in egg, then vanilla. Reduce mixer speed to low and beat in flour mixture, just until blended. Using a wooden spoon, stir in chocolate chips, coconut, and pecans.

3. Transfer mixture to prepared pan and press down evenly with the back of a wooden spoon. Bake 20 to 25 minutes, until top is dry and golden brown, and a toothpick inserted in the center comes out with a moist crumb. Cool completely on a wire cake rack.

MAKES 24 BLONDIES

 ADRIENNE'S INCREDIBLE MICROWAVE BROWNIES

Yes, you can bake brownies in a microwave oven. Adrienne Welch, who, with Mary Goodbody, is currently writing a book on microwave baking and desserts (Simon & Schuster, 1991), has given us this recipe. This brownie uses corn syrup to lock in moistness during baking and cocoa and chocolate chips for intense chocolate flavor.

1 cup sifted all-purpose flour	¼ cup light corn syrup
½ cup unsweetened alkalized cocoa powder, such as Droste	2 large eggs, at room temperature
½ teaspoon baking powder	2 teaspoons vanilla extract
⅛ teaspoon salt	3 ounces walnuts, coarsely chopped (about ¾ cup)
8 tablespoons (1 stick) unsalted butter, cut into pieces	1 cup semisweet chocolate chips (1 6-ounce package)
¾ cup granulated sugar	

1. In a medium bowl, whisk flour, cocoa, baking powder, and salt to combine. Place butter in a 3-quart microwave-proof bowl. Microwave uncovered at defrost (30-percent power) for 45 to 55 seconds just until soft; do not let butter melt.

2. Using a hand-held electric mixer set at high speed, beat softened butter, sugar, and corn syrup for 45 seconds, until creamy. One at a time, beat in eggs, then vanilla. At low speed, beat in flour-cocoa mixture. Stir in ½ cup of walnuts.

3. Spread batter evenly into an 8-inch square microwave-proof glass baking dish. Wrap the four corners of the dish with 1¼-inch-wide strips of aluminum foil, and elevate the baking dish on a shallow microwave-proof bowl in the center of the oven.

4. Microwave uncovered on medium (50-percent power) for 3 minutes, then rotate the brownie dish one-quarter turn. Remove foil strips, and microwave 2 minutes. Continue cooking for 5 to 7 minutes, rotating the dish one-quarter turn every 2 minutes. (If your microwave has a turntable, the rotating is unnecessary.) Start testing for doneness after a total cooking time of 8 minutes; a toothpick inserted 1 inch from the side of the dish should come out clean. (Any moist spots on the top of the brownie will dry upon standing.)

5. Remove brownie dish and place on flat heatproof surface. Sprinkle chocolate chips evenly over top of brownie. Let brownie stand 10 minutes. With a metal cake spatula, spread softened chips gently and evenly over brownie; then sprinkle on remaining ¼ cup of walnuts. Cool brownie completely at room temperature before cutting into squares.

MAKES 12 BROWNIES

(Note: this recipe was tested in a 700-watt microwave oven. Adjust cooking times for smaller models.)

FLO'S WHITE CHOCOLATE RASPBERRY BROWNIE PETITS FOURS

Flo Braker, cookbook author and teacher extraordinaire, shares her favorite sophisticated and original recipe for dark, rich fudge brownies topped with white chocolate–covered fresh red raspberries.

RASPBERRY BROWNIE

¾ cup all-purpose flour
¼ teaspoon baking soda
⅛ teaspoon salt
6 tablespoons (¾ stick) unsalted butter, cut into pieces
3 ounces unsweetened chocolate, finely chopped
½ cup granulated sugar

½ cup packed light brown sugar
1 tablespoon light corn syrup
2 large eggs, at room temperature
2 teaspoons vanilla extract
½ cup fresh red raspberries, at room temperature

WHITE CHOCOLATE RASPBERRY TOPPING

4 tablespoons (½ stick) unsalted butter, cut into pieces
6 ounces white chocolate, chopped fine
½ cup fresh red raspberries, at room temperature

1. *Brownie:* Position a rack in the lower third of the oven and preheat to 325°F. Line an 8-inch square baking pan with a double thickness of aluminum foil so that the foil extends 2 inches beyond two of the opposite ends of the pan. Fold the overhang down to form "handles." Butter the bottom of the foil-lined pan. Sift flour, baking soda, and salt through a wire strainer onto a sheet of wax paper.

2. In a medium saucepan over low heat, melt butter. Off heat, add chocolate and let stand 1 minute; whisk until smooth. Pour into a large bowl, and let stand 5 minutes, until tepid. Whisk in sugars and corn syrup. Whisk in eggs, then vanilla. Using a wooden spoon, stir in flour mixture, just until blended. Using a rubber spatula, carefully fold in raspberries.

3. Spread batter evenly into prepared pan and bake 25 to 30 minutes, until a toothpick inserted 1 inch from the edge of the brownie comes out with a moist crumb.

Cool on a wire cake rack for 10 minutes. Invert onto the wire cake rack, carefully peel off aluminum foil, and cool completely.

4. *White Chocolate Raspberry Topping:* In the top part of a double boiler, over hot, not simmering, water, melt butter. (Water should be no warmer than 125° F.) Add white chocolate and melt, stirring often until smooth. Transfer to a small bowl, and let stand 10 minutes, until tepid and slightly thickened. Using a metal cake spatula, spread half of the topping onto the top of the brownie. Freeze brownie for 5 minutes, just until topping is partially set. Using a sharp knife, mark topping of brownie into 16 squares. Using a rubber spatula, carefully fold remaining ½ raspberries into remaining topping. Divide white chocolate–coated raspberries evenly among brownies, arranging them attractively on top of each square. Loosely cover brownies with plastic wrap, and refrigerate for 30 minutes to set topping completely. Using a sharp knife, cut through markings into 16 squares. Transfer brownies to a serving plate and cover tightly with plastic wrap. Brownies can be made up to 1 day ahead, refrigerated, and covered with plastic wrap. Bring to room temperature before serving.

MAKES 16 BROWNIE PETITS FOURS

BARB'S FUDGY
FOOD-PROCESSOR BROWNIES

As editor-in-chief of Chocolatier *magazine, Barbara Albright gets to taste all the brownies she could ever want. But when she dashes home from a long day of chocolate tasting and aerobics, she uses her food processor to help whip up her own favorite time-saving dishes.*

8 tablespoons (1 stick) unsalted butter, cut into pieces
½ cup packed light brown sugar
¼ cup granulated sugar

9 ounces European bittersweet chocolate, broken into pieces
1 ounce unsweetened chocolate
2 large eggs, at room temperature

1½ teaspoons vanilla extract
½ cup all-purpose flour
⅛ teaspoon salt
4 ounces walnuts (about 1 cup)

1. Position a rack in the center of the oven and preheat to 350°F. Line an 8-inch square baking pan with a double thickness of aluminum foil so that the foil extends 2 inches over two opposite ends of the pan. Fold the overhang down to form "handles." Butter the bottom of the foil-lined pan.

2. In a medium saucepan over medium heat, combine butter and sugars and cook, stirring constantly, 4 to 6 minutes, until the butter is melted. Remove from heat.

3. Place both chocolates in a food processor fitted with the metal chopping blade. Process chocolates for 15 to 20 seconds, until finely chopped. Add hot butter/sugar mixture and process 15 to 20 seconds, scraping down work bowl as necessary. Add eggs and vanilla, and process 10 to 15 seconds, until combined. Add flour and salt and process 5 to 7 seconds, just until combined, scraping down work bowl as necessary. Add walnuts, and pulse 10 times to chop slightly.

4. Spread batter evenly into prepared pan and bake 25 to 30 minutes, until a toothpick inserted 2 inches in center of brownie comes out with a slightly moist crumb. *Do not overbake.* Cool for 30 minutes on a wire cake rack. Lift up on foil "handles" to remove brownie from pan. Cool completely on foil on the wire cake rack. Invert brownie onto a large plate and carefully peel off foil. Invert again and cut into 16 squares.

MAKES 16 BROWNIES

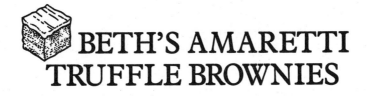

BETH'S AMARETTI TRUFFLE BROWNIES

Brownies with an Italian flair, created by Beth Hensperger, one of the San Francisco Bay Area's favorite caterers and cooking teachers. Her brownies are on the sweet side and explode with flavors Italians love so well.

10 amaretti cookies (or 5 wrapped pairs)
8 tablespoons (1 stick) unsalted butter, cut into pieces
4 ounces bittersweet chocolate, finely chopped
3 large eggs, at room temperature
¾ cup granulated sugar
1½ tablespoons Amaretto liqueur
1 teaspoon vanilla extract
¾ cup all-purpose flour
⅛ teaspoon salt
Confectioners' sugar, for dusting

1. Position a rack in the center of the oven and preheat to 350°F. Line the bottom of a 9-inch square baking pan with wax paper and lightly butter the sides of the pan. Place amaretti cookies in a food processor fitted with the metal blade and process for 20 seconds, until finely ground, to yield ¼ cup ground amaretti crumbs.

2. In a medium saucepan over low heat, melt butter. Off heat, add chocolate and let stand 1 minute; whisk until smooth. Let stand 10 minutes, until tepid.

3. In a large bowl, using a hand-held electric mixer set at high speed, beat eggs and sugar for 3 minutes, until thickened and very light in color. Beat in Amaretto and vanilla. Reduce speed to low and beat in melted chocolate mixture, just until blended. Beat in flour, ground cookies, and salt, just until blended.

4. Spread batter evenly into prepared pan and bake 22 to 27 minutes, until a toothpick inserted in the center of the brownie comes out with a moist crumb. Cool completely on a wire cake rack. Invert brownie onto a large plate and carefully peel off wax paper. Invert again onto another plate, cover tightly with plastic wrap, and refrigerate at least 4 hours, or overnight. To garnish, sift confectioners' sugar through a wire strainer over top of brownie.

MAKES 12 BROWNIES

BEVERLY'S CHEWIES

Dear friend and dessert lover Beverly Moody shared this easy hand-me-down family recipe for the chewiest butterscotch blondies. While baking, the chewies smell like Christmas. While rolling them, it is fun to munch on scraps that "accidentally" fall into the confectioners' sugar. While eating them, the name says it all. (We swear there is no butter in this recipe!)

2 large eggs, at room
    temperature
1¾ cups packed light brown
    sugar
1 cup all-purpose flour

⅛ teaspoon baking soda
4 ounces walnuts, coarsely
    chopped (about 1 cup)
Confectioners' sugar, sifted, for
    rolling

1. Position a rack in the center of the oven and preheat to 350°F. Line an 8″ × 12″ baking pan with a double thickness of aluminum foil so that the foil extends 2 inches beyond the shorts ends of the pan. Fold the overhang down to form "handles." Lightly butter the bottom and sides of the foil-lined pan.

2. In a medium bowl, whisk eggs for 30 seconds, just until lightly beaten. Whisk in brown sugar until combined. (If you have any lumps in your brown sugar, press them out now against the side of the bowl with a wooden spoon.) Using a wooden spoon, stir in flour, baking soda, and walnuts to form a stiff, sticky mixture.

3. Using a rubber spatula, press mixture evenly into prepared pan and spread into corners. Bake 25 to 30 minutes, just until the top is golden brown and a toothpick inserted in the center comes out clean. *Do not overbake.* Cool on a wire cake rack for 1 hour, until slightly warm. Run a knife around the inside edges of the pan to release brownie from the sides. Lift up on the "handles" to remove brownie. Using a sharp knife, cut into 24 strips. (The tops of the chewies will crack, but don't be concerned, as they will be rolled in confectioners' sugar.)

4. Place the confectioners' sugar in a medium bowl. A few at a time, roll the chewies in the confectioners' sugar to coat. Chewies are best eaten immediately, but can be stored, tightly wrapped in plastic, at room temperature for up to 24 hours.

MAKES 24 CHEWIES

BROWNIE MUFFINS

Finally—brownies for breakfast! We enjoy our morning muffin fix slathered with red raspberry jam.

BROWNIE MUFFINS
1 cup all-purpose flour
¾ cup granulated sugar
¼ cup unsweetened nonalkalized cocoa powder, such as Hershey's
1 teaspoon baking powder
¼ teaspoon baking soda
½ teaspoon salt

½ cup buttermilk, at room temperature
4 tablespoons (½ stick) unsalted butter, melted
1 large egg, lightly beaten, at room temperature
1 teaspoon vanilla extract

STREUSEL TOPPING
1 ounce walnuts, coarsely chopped (about ¼ cup)
2 tablespoons light brown sugar
2 tablespoons all-purpose flour
1 tablespoon unsalted butter, melted

1. *Muffins:* Position a rack in the center of the oven and preheat to 350°F. Lightly butter and flour 8 muffin molds, each 2¾″ × 1¼″, with a 3-ounce capacity, tapping out excess flour.

2. Sift flour, sugar, cocoa, baking powder, baking soda, and salt through a wire strainer into a medium bowl. In another bowl, stir together buttermilk, butter, egg, and vanilla. Make a well in the center of the flour mixture, pour in liquid mixture, and stir with a wooden spoon just until blended. Do not overmix.

3. Divide batter between prepared molds, using about 2 heaping tablespoons per muffin. Do not fill the molds more than two-thirds full.

4. *Streusel:* In a small bowl, combine walnuts, sugar, flour, and butter until well mixed and crumbly. Sprinkle streusel evenly over tops of muffins. Bake 18 to 20 minutes, until tops of muffins spring back when lightly touched. Cool muffins in pan set on a wire cake rack for 5 minutes. Serve warm.

MAKES 8 MUFFINS

GINGERED APPLESAUCE BROWNIE SQUARES

A perfect wintertime hostess gift, a delightful brownie tea cake, and a delicious carry-along snack cake all in one. Try serving this thick and subtly spiced brownie warm as a cold weather dessert, accompanied by sweetened whipped cream.

8 tablespoons (1 stick) unsalted butter, cut into pieces
2 ounces unsweetened chocolate, finely chopped
1 cup granulated sugar
1 large egg, at room temperature

1 teaspoon vanilla extract
1 cup all-purpose flour
¾ cup sweetened applesauce, store-bought or homemade
1 teaspoon baking powder
¼ teaspoon ground ginger
½ teaspoon ground cinnamon

¼ teaspoon salt
2 tablespoons finely chopped crystallized ginger
1 7-inch paper doily, for decorating
Confectioners' sugar for dusting

1. Position a rack in the center of the oven and preheat to 350°F. Line an 8-inch square baking pan with a double thickness of aluminum foil so that the foil extends 2 inches over two opposite ends of the pan. Fold the overhang down to form "handles." Butter the bottom of the foil-lined pan.

2. In a medium saucepan over low heat, melt butter. Off heat, add chocolate and let stand 1 minute; whisk until smooth. Let stand 10 minutes, until tepid. Whisk in sugar. Whisk in egg, then vanilla. Using a wooden spoon, stir in flour, applesauce, baking powder, ground ginger, cinnamon, and salt, just until blended. Stir in crystallized ginger.

3. Spread batter evenly into prepared pan. Bake 25 to 30 minutes, until a toothpick inserted in the center comes out clean. Cool completely on a wire cake rack.

4. To decorate, place a doily on top of the brownie. Sift confectioners' sugar over top of doily and brownie. Carefully lift doily, and decorative lacy sugar pattern will remain.

MAKES 12 BROWNIES

RASPBERRY TRUFFLED BROWNIES

A sophisticated brownie dessert experience—a fudgelike brownie bursting with fresh, plump, red raspberries and a creamy bittersweet ganache. True perfection.

BROWNIE
1 cup all-purpose flour
¼ teaspoon baking soda
¼ teaspoon salt
8 tablespoons (1 stick) unsalted butter, cut into pieces
6 ounces European bittersweet chocolate, finely chopped
1 cup granulated sugar

2 large eggs, at room temperature
1 teaspoon vanilla extract
½ cup fresh red raspberries, or ½ cup frozen raspberries, thawed, without syrup, well drained on paper towels

TRUFFLE FROSTING
¾ cup heavy cream
6 ounces European bittersweet chocolate, finely chopped
2 tablespoons seedless red raspberry preserves
12 fresh whole red raspberries, for garnish

1. *Brownie:* Position a rack in the center of the oven and preheat to 350°F. Lightly butter and flour a 9-inch square baking pan, tapping out excess flour. Sift flour, baking soda, and salt through a wire strainer onto a sheet of wax paper.

2. In a small saucepan over low heat, melt butter. Off heat, add chocolate and let stand 1 minute; whisk until smooth. Cool 10 minutes, until tepid.

3. In a medium bowl, whisk together sugar and eggs, just until blended. Whisk in chocolate mixture. Add vanilla. Using a wooden spoon, stir in flour mixture, just until blended. Carefully fold in raspberries.

4. Spread batter evenly into prepared pan and bake 25 to 30 minutes, until a toothpick inserted in the center comes out with a moist crumb. Cool completely on a wire cake rack.

5. *Truffle Frosting:* In a small saucepan over low heat, bring cream to a low simmer. Off heat, add chocolate and preserves and let stand 1 minute to melt chocolate; whisk until smooth. Transfer mixture to a medium bowl set in a larger bowl of iced water. Let mixture set 3 to 5 minutes, until cool, whisking occasionally. Whisk cooled chocolate mixture just until soft peaks form.

6. Transfer ½ cup of frosting to a pastry bag fitted with a large star tip. Spread remaining frosting evenly over top of cooled brownie. Cut brownie into twelve squares. Pipe a rosette of frosting in the center of each square, and top each rosette with a fresh raspberry. Refrigerate brownies about 30 minutes, until frosting is firm. Store brownies covered and refrigerated.

MAKES 12 BROWNIES

 # PATCHWORK BROWNIES

Visually stunning, this exceptionally light brownie is created from chocolate-chip blondie and chocolate-nut brownie doughs which are arranged to form a crisscross pattern. Confectioners' sugar and cocoa-powder stripes enhance the dazzling presentation.

2 ounces unsweetened chocolate, finely chopped
8 tablespoons (1 stick) unsalted butter, cut into pieces
1 cup granulated sugar
2 large eggs, at room temperature
1 teaspoon vanilla extract
1 cup all-purpose flour
1 teaspoon baking powder
¼ teaspoon salt

1 ounce walnuts, finely chopped (about ¼ cup)
¼ cup semisweet chocolate chips (about 1½ ounces)
½ cup (approximately) confectioners' sugar, for garnish
⅓ cup (approximately) unsweetened cocoa powder, for garnish

1. Position a rack in the center of the oven and preheat to 350°F. Lightly butter and flour an 8-inch square baking pan, tapping out excess flour.

2. In the top part of a double boiler, over hot, not simmering, water, melt chocolate, stirring often, until smooth. Remove from heat and cool 10 minutes, until tepid.

3. In a medium saucepan over low heat, melt butter. Off heat, whisk in sugar. One at a time, whisk in eggs, then vanilla. Using a wooden spoon, stir in flour, baking powder, and salt, just until blended. Divide batter evenly between two medium bowls. In one bowl, stir in cooled chocolate and walnuts. In the second bowl, stir in chocolate chips.

4. Arrange five alternating diagonal rows of dark and white batters in the prepared pan by spooning the batter in rows about 2 inches wide. (Start by filling in the bottom left-hand corner of the pan with a triangle of dark batter.) Using a metal cake spatula, carefully smooth the top of the batter, keeping the rows as distinct as possible. Bake 22 to 27 minutes, until a toothpick inserted 1 inch from the edge of the brownie comes out with a moist crumb. Cool completely on a wire cake rack.

5. Cut four strips of wax paper, 12 inches long by 1½ inches wide. Place strips diagonally on top of the brownie, running in the opposite direction of the angle of the dark and white brownie rows, leaving a 1½-inch space between the strips. Sift the confectioners' sugar over the rows of brownie that are exposed between the wax-paper strips. Carefully lift the wax-paper strips, leaving rows of confectioner's sugar on the brownie. Repeat the procedure by "crisscrossing" the wax-paper strips in the opposite direction over the top of the confectioners' sugar, and sifting cocoa powder over the exposed areas. Using a serrated knife, cut the brownie into 12 squares.

MAKES 12 BROWNIES

RAINBOW BROWNIES

Way, way under the rainbow is a thin chocolate crisp crust. Next comes a chewy white chocolate brownie sprinkled with a haze of M&M's in every hue.

COOKIE CRUST
3 tablespoons unsalted butter
1 cup crushed chocolate wafer
  cookies (about 4 ounces)
3 tablespoons granulated sugar

WHITE CHOCOLATE BROWNIE
3 ounces white chocolate, finely
  chopped
6 tablespoons (¾ stick) unsalted
  butter, at room temperature
1 cup granulated sugar
2 large eggs, at room
  temperature
1 teaspoon vanilla extract
1¼ cups all-purpose flour
¼ teaspoon baking powder
¼ teaspoon salt
½ cup M&M's

1. *Cookie Crust:* Position a rack in the center of the oven and preheat to 350°F. Line an 8-inch square baking pan with a double thickness of aluminum foil so that the foil extends 2 inches over two opposite ends of the pan. Fold the overhang down to form "handles." Butter the bottom of the foil-lined pan.

2. In a medium saucepan over low heat, melt butter. Off heat, stir in crushed cookies and sugar until well combined. Press cookie mixture evenly into bottom of prepared pan.

3. *Brownie:* In the top part of a double boiler, over hot water, melt half the white chocolate, stirring often, until almost smooth. (Water should be no warmer than 125°F.) Add the remaining white chocolate and melt, stirring often, until completely smooth. Remove from heat; let stand 10 minutes, until tepid.

4. In a medium bowl, using a hand-held electric mixer set at high speed, beat butter and sugar about 2 minutes, until light in color and texture. One at a time, beat in eggs, then vanilla. Beat in cooled white chocolate. Using a wooden spoon, stir in flour, baking powder, and salt.

5. Spread batter evenly into prepared pan and sprinkle M&M's over the top.

Bake 30 to 35 minutes, until a toothpick inserted in the center comes out with a moist crumb. Cool completely on a wire cake rack. Run a knife around the inside edges of the pan to release brownie from sides. Lift up on foil "handles" to remove brownie from pan.

MAKES 16 BROWNIES

ST. VALENTINE'S STRAWBERRY BROWNIE HEARTS

Gleaming with a bittersweet glaze, these gorgeous treats will be sure to win your valentine's heart. As a bonus, you will have trimmings from cutting out the heart shapes, which can be used in Chocolate-Chocolate Brownie Chunk Cheesecake, Brownie Chunk Ice Cream, or Layered Brownie Fudge Pudding Parfaits (see Index).

BROWNIE HEARTS

12 tablespoons (1½ sticks) unsalted butter, cut into pieces
6 ounces unsweetened chocolate, finely chopped
6 large eggs, at room temperature
2 cups granulated sugar
2 teaspoons vanilla extract
1¾ cups all-purpose flour
½ teaspoon salt
½ cup strawberry jelly

GLAZE

1¼ cups heavy cream
12 ounces bittersweet or semisweet chocolate, finely chopped
3 tablespoons strawberry jelly
14 fresh strawberries, sliced into fan shapes, for garnish

    1. *Brownie Hearts:* Position a rack in the center of the oven and preheat to 350°F. Line an 11″ × 17″ jelly-roll pan with a double thickness of aluminum foil so that the foil extends 2 inches beyond the two short ends of the pan. Fold the overhang down to form "handles." Butter the bottom of the foil-lined pan.
    2. In a medium saucepan over low heat, melt butter. Off heat, add unsweet-

81

ened chocolate and let stand 1 minute; whisk until smooth. Let stand 10 minutes, until tepid.

3. In a large bowl, using a hand-held electric mixer set at high speed, beat eggs and sugar for 3 minutes, until thick and very light in color. Beat in chocolate mixture, then vanilla. Using a wooden spoon, beat in flour and salt, just until blended.

4. Spread batter evenly into prepared pan and bake 12 to 15 minutes, just until a toothpick inserted in the center comes out clean. *Do not overbake.* Cool completely on a wire cake rack. Run a knife around the inside edges of the pan to release brownie from sides. Lift up on "handles" to remove brownie. Place brownie on a flat working surface. Using a 3-inch heart-shaped cookie cutter, cut out 14 hearts. (Trimmings can be saved, frozen, and used in other recipes, as described above.) Place the hearts on a wire cake rack set over a wax paper–lined work surface. In a small saucepan over low heat, heat jelly, stirring, until melted. Brush melted jelly over tops of hearts.

5. *Glaze:* In a medium saucepan over low heat, bring cream to a low simmer. Off heat, add bittersweet chocolate and strawberry jelly and let stand 2 minutes; whisk until smooth. Transfer to a medium bowl and let stand 10 minutes, until tepid and slightly thickened. Spoon about 3 tablespoons of glaze over the top of each brownie heart. Using a metal cake spatula, smooth glaze over top of brownie, letting excess run down sides. Pick up any excess glaze on the wax paper with the spatula, and use it to cover any bare spots. Place a strawberry fan on top of each heart. Transfer brownie hearts to two baking sheets and refrigerate for 30 minutes to set glaze. Brownie hearts can be made up to 1 day ahead, covered tightly with plastic wrap, and refrigerated on the baking sheets.

MAKES 14 3-INCH HEARTS

MINTY CREAM CHIP BROWNIES

The coolest brownie combination we know. A refreshing frosting, infused with crème de menthe, is generously slathered on a fudgy brownie base, then sprinkled with miniature chocolate chips.

BROWNIE

8 tablespoons (1 stick) unsalted butter, cut into pieces
2 ounces unsweetened chocolate, finely chopped
1 cup packed light brown sugar
2 large eggs, at room temperature
1 tablespoon green crème de menthe liqueur
½ teaspoon vanilla extract
⅔ cup all-purpose flour
¼ teaspoon salt

FROSTING

1½ cups confectioners' sugar, sifted
3 tablespoons unsalted butter, at room temperature
2 tablespoons green crème de menthe liqueur
½ cup miniature semisweet chocolate chips

1. *Brownie:* Position a rack in the center of the oven and preheat to 350°F. Lightly butter an 8-inch square baking pan.

2. In a medium saucepan over low heat, melt butter. Off heat, add chocolate and let stand 1 minute; whisk until smooth. Let stand 10 minutes, until tepid. Whisk in brown sugar. One at a time, whisk in eggs, then the crème de menthe and vanilla. Using a wooden spoon, stir in flour and salt, just until blended.

3. Spread batter evenly into prepared pan and bake 20 to 25 minutes, until a toothpick inserted in the center comes out with a moist crumb. Cool completely on a wire cake rack.

4. *Frosting:* In a medium bowl, using a hand-held electric mixer set at medium speed, beat confectioners' sugar, butter, and crème de menthe for 1 minute, until fluffy. Spread frosting evenly over top of brownie, sprinkle with chocolate chips, and refrigerate for about 1 hour, until frosting is firm.

MAKES 16 BROWNIES

PRUNE-ARMAGNAC BROWNIES

A high-spirited brownie with a shiny, bittersweet chocolate glaze. The prunes are steeped in Armagnac, a heady brandy made from a wine from Gascony, and stirred into a deep, dark batter. Age these for a day or two, wrapped in plastic and refrigerated, for a more intense flavor and a texture reminiscent of a fine French bonbon.

BROWNIE
½ cup chopped pitted prunes
2 tablespoons Armagnac, Cognac, or brandy
7 tablespoons unsalted butter, cut into pieces
4 ounces bittersweet chocolate, finely chopped

¾ cup granulated sugar
2 large eggs, at room temperature
1 teaspoon vanilla extract
⅔ cup all-purpose flour
¼ teaspoon baking soda
¼ teaspoon salt

GLAZE
¼ cup heavy cream
4 ounces bittersweet chocolate, finely chopped

Chocolate leaves, for garnish (see Index)

1. *Brownie:* In a small bowl, combine prunes and Armagnac; let stand at room temperature for 2 hours, or overnight.

2. Position a rack in the center of the oven and preheat to 350°F. Line an 8-inch square baking pan with a double thickness of aluminum foil so that the foil extends 2 inches over two opposite ends of the pan. Fold the overhang down to form "handles." Butter the bottom of the foil-lined pan.

3. In a medium saucepan over low heat, melt butter. Off heat, add chocolate and let stand 1 minute; whisk until smooth. Whisk in sugar. One at a time, whisk in eggs, then vanilla. Using a wooden spoon, stir in flour, baking soda, and salt. Stir in prunes and Armagnac.

4. Spread batter evenly into prepared pan and bake 22 to 28 minutes, until a toothpick inserted 1 inch from the center comes out with a moist crumb. Cool completely on a wire cake rack. Remove brownie from pan by lifting up on foil "handles."

5. *Glaze:* In a small saucepan over low heat, bring cream to a simmer. Off heat, add chocolate and let stand 1 minute; whisk until smooth. Transfer to a small bowl and let stand 10 minutes, until tepid. Using a metal cake spatula, spread glaze thinly over top of brownie. Cut brownie into 12 squares, and top each with a chocolate leaf.

MAKES 12 BROWNIES

PEANUT-BUTTER-AND-JELLY BARS

A childhood favorite: chunky peanut-butter-and-grape-jelly sandwich minus the Wonder Bread. Half the brownie is baked briefly, then layered with a peanut-butter-and-jelly filling, and covered with the remaining peanut butter batter. These brownies are best when eaten within twenty-four hours of baking.

PEANUT-BUTTER-AND-JELLY FILLING
¼ cup grape jelly
¼ cup chunky peanut butter

PEANUT BUTTER BROWNIE
⅓ cup chunky peanut butter
4 tablespoons (½ stick) unsalted butter, at room temperature
1 cup packed light brown sugar
2 large eggs, at room temperature

1 teaspoon vanilla extract
¾ cup all-purpose flour
1 teaspoon baking powder
¼ teaspoon salt

1. *Filling:* In a small saucepan over low heat, heat jelly just until warm. Off heat, stir in peanut butter, until barely combined.
2. *Brownie:* Position a rack in the center of the oven and preheat to 350°F. Line an 8-inch square baking pan with a double thickness of aluminum foil so that the foil

85

extends 2 inches over two opposite ends of the pan. Fold the overhang down to form "handles." Butter the bottom of the foil-lined pan.

3. In a medium bowl, using a hand-held electric mixer set at high speed, beat peanut butter and butter about 1 minute, until well combined. Add brown sugar and beat 2 to 3 minutes, until very light in color. One at a time, beat in eggs, then vanilla. Using a wooden spoon, stir in flour, baking powder, and salt, just until blended.

4. Spread half of the batter evenly into the prepared pan and bake about 7 minutes, just until set. Drop peanut-butter-and-jelly filling by large tablespoons over surface of brownie, and using a metal spatula, carefully spread filling over surface. (Don't worry if filling sinks slightly into batter.) Using a large spoon, spoon remaining batter over filling, spreading batter carefully.

5. Bake 22 to 28 minutes, until a toothpick inserted halfway down into the center of the brownie, just short of the filling, comes out clean. Cool completely on a wire cake rack.

MAKES 16 BROWNIES

 # GRANOLA BROWNIE SQUARES

These extraordinary chewy granola squares are very thin, with a rich honey-almond flavor. And they're wheat-free and made without eggs!

11 tablespoons (1 stick plus 3 tablespoons) unsalted butter, cut into pieces	⅓ cup honey
	½ teaspoon salt
	½ teaspoon almond extract
½ cup unsweetened nonalkalized cocoa powder, such as Hershey's	1 cup slivered almonds
	1 cup dark raisins
	4 cups old-fashioned rolled oats
1 cup packed light brown sugar	(*not* quick-cooking oats)

1. Position a rack in the center of the oven and preheat to 350°F. Line a 10″ × 15″ jelly-roll pan with a double thickness of aluminum foil so that the foil extends 2 inches beyond the two short ends of the pan. Fold the overhang down to form "handles." Lightly butter and flour the foil-lined pan, tapping out excess flour.

2. In a large saucepan over medium heat, melt butter. Remove the pan from the heat and whisk in cocoa, until smooth. Using a wooden spoon, stir in brown sugar, honey, salt, almond extract, slivered almonds, raisins, and oats, just until blended.

3. Spread batter evenly into prepared jelly-roll pan and bake 20 to 25 minutes, until the entire surface of the brownie is bubbling gently. *Do not overbake.* (Brownie may seem liquid, but will firm upon standing.) Cool completely on a wire cake rack.

MAKES 24 BROWNIES

WHITE-ON-WHITE FANTASY BROWNIES

Some like it white. This creamy white chocolate–glazed golden brownie is dedicated to those who enjoy sweet desserts.

BROWNIE
6 tablespoons (¾ stick) unsalted
   butter, cut into pieces
3 ounces white chocolate, finely
   chopped
1 cup granulated sugar
2 large eggs, at room
   temperature

1 teaspoon vanilla extract
1¼ cups all-purpose flour
¼ teaspoon baking powder
¼ teaspoon salt

WHITE CHOCOLATE GLAZE
⅓ cup heavy cream
6 ounces white chocolate, finely
   chopped

1. *Brownie:* Position a rack in the center of the oven and preheat to 350°F. Lightly butter and flour the bottom of an 8-inch square baking pan, tapping out excess flour.

2. In the top part of a double boiler, over hot, not simmering, water, melt butter. (Water should be no warmer than 125°F.) Add half of the white chocolate and let stand 1 or 2 minutes; then whisk until almost smooth. Add remaining white chocolate and melt, whisking often until smooth. Transfer to a medium bowl and let stand 10 minutes, until tepid. Whisk in sugar. One at a time, whisk in eggs, then vanilla. Using a wooden spoon, stir in flour, baking powder, and salt, just until blended.

3. Spread batter evenly into prepared pan and bake 25 to 30 minutes, until a toothpick inserted in the center comes out clean. Cool completely on a wire cake rack.

4. *Glaze:* In the top part of a double boiler, over hot, not simmering, water, heat cream. (Water should be no warmer than 125°F.) Add half of the white chocolate and whisk until almost smooth. Add remaining white chocolate and whisk again until smooth. Transfer to a medium bowl and let stand 15 minutes, until tepid and slightly

thickened. Using a metal cake spatula, spread glaze evenly over top of brownie. Cover loosely with plastic wrap and refrigerate 30 minutes to set glaze.

MAKES 12 BROWNIES

 # CRANBERRY HOLIDAY BROWNIE FUDGE

Each holiday season, we engage in the annual debate over jellied versus whole cranberry sauce, and the whole-cranberry purists usually win. So, we've created a combination brownie/confection/fudge—rich, dense, and chocolaty with whole cranberries and a festive glaze.

9 tablespoons (1 stick plus 1 tablespoon) unsalted butter, cut into pieces
6 ounces semisweet chocolate, finely chopped
¾ cup granulated sugar

2 large eggs, at room temperature
1 teaspoon vanilla extract
1 16-ounce can whole-berry cranberry sauce, divided

1 cup all-purpose flour
¼ teaspoon salt
4 ounces walnuts, coarsely chopped (about 1 cup)

1. Position a rack in the center of the oven and preheat to 350°F. Line an 8-inch square baking pan with a double thickness of aluminum foil so that the foil extends 2 inches over two opposite ends of the pan. Fold the overhang down to form "handles." Butter the foil-lined pan.

2. In a medium saucepan over low heat, melt butter. Off heat, add chocolate and let stand 1 minute; whisk until smooth. Let stand 10 minutes, until tepid. Whisk in sugar. One at a time, whisk in eggs, then vanilla. Whisk in ¾ cup cranberry sauce. Using a wooden spoon, stir in flour and salt, just until blended. Stir in walnuts.

3. Spread batter evenly into prepared pan and bake 22 to 27 minutes, until a toothpick inserted in the center comes out with a moist crumb. Cool completely on a wire cake rack.

4. In a small bowl, using a wooden spoon, stir remaining cranberry sauce until loosened and spreadable. Spread brownie with cranberry sauce, cover tightly with plastic wrap, and refrigerate overnight. Run a knife around inside edges of pan to release brownie from sides. Lift up on the "handles" to remove the brownie, and then cut it into 24 squares. Cover loosely with plastic wrap and store, refrigerated for up to 3 days. These brownies are best when eaten chilled.

MAKES 24 BROWNIES

 # COFFEE-AND-CREAM BROWNIES

Coffee liqueur heightens the intensity of the chocolate flavor, and a cream-cheese swirl adds moistness and a vivid contrast. These chewy brownies taste as luscious as they look.

BROWNIES

6 tablespoons (¾ stick) unsalted butter, cut into pieces
3 ounces unsweetened chocolate, finely chopped
1½ teaspoons instant espresso powder
2 large eggs, at room temperature

1 cup granulated sugar
2 tablespoons coffee-flavored liqueur, such as Kahlua
½ teaspoon vanilla extract
½ cup all-purpose flour
¼ teaspoon baking soda
⅛ teaspoon salt

CREAM-CHEESE SWIRL

3 ounces cream cheese, softened
⅓ cup granulated sugar
1 large egg yolk, at room temperature
2 tablespoons coffee-flavored liqueur, such as Kahlua

1. *Brownie:* Position a rack in the center of the oven and preheat to 350°F. Lightly butter and flour an 8-inch square baking pan, tapping out excess flour.

2. In a medium saucepan over low heat, melt butter. Off heat, add chocolate and espresso powder and let stand 1 minute; whisk until smooth. Cool 10 minutes, until tepid.

3. In a medium bowl, using a hand-held electric mixer set at high speed, mix eggs and sugar for 2 minutes, until thickened and light in color. Beat in chocolate mixture, coffee liqueur, and vanilla. Using a wooden spoon, stir in flour, baking soda, and salt, just until combined. Spread batter evenly into prepared pan.

4. *Cream-Cheese Swirl:* In a small bowl, using a hand-held electric mixer set at medium speed, beat cream cheese and sugar for 1 minute, until very smooth. Beat in egg yolk and coffee liqueur. Drop filling by tablespoons over chocolate batter. Draw a dinner knife through the two batters, swirling them together for a marbleized effect.

5. Bake 28 to 33 minutes, until a toothpick inserted in the center comes out with a moist crumb. Cool completely on a wire cake rack.

MAKES 12 BROWNIES

CANDY BAR BROWNIES

Craving a midafternoon snack, and can't decide between your favorite candy bar or a chewy chocolaty brownie? Chop your favorite candy bar into a batch of quick 'n' easy brownies and enjoy the best of both. We like Butterfingers and Heath Bars best.

6 tablespoons (¾ stick) unsalted butter, cut into pieces

3 ounces unsweetened chocolate, finely chopped

1 cup granulated sugar

2 large eggs, at room temperature

1 teaspoon vanilla extract

⅔ cup all-purpose flour

¼ teaspoon baking soda

¼ teaspoon salt

2 Heath Bars, 1.60 ounces each, cut into chunks about ½ inch square (about ½ cup) **or** 2 Butterfinger Bars, 2.01 ounces each, cut into chunks about ½ inch square (about ¾ cup)

1. Position a rack in the center of the oven and preheat to 350°F. Lightly butter and flour an 8-inch square baking pan, tapping out excess flour.

2. In a medium saucepan over low heat, melt butter. Off heat, add chocolate and let stand 1 minute; whisk until smooth. Let stand 10 minutes, until tepid. Whisk in sugar. One at a time, whisk in eggs, then vanilla. Using a wooden spoon, stir in flour, baking soda, and salt. Stir in chopped candy bar chunks.

3. Spread batter evenly into prepared pan and bake 20 to 25 minutes, until a toothpick inserted 1 inch from the edge of the brownie comes out with a moist crumb. Cool completely on a wire cake rack.

MAKES 16 BROWNIES

# CAMPSITE RAISIN BROWNIES

A dense, not-too-sweet brownie packed with chewy raisins. The perfect carry-along treat for bike rides or camping trips—these brownies taste even fudgier a day after baking.

BROWNIE
1 cup packed light brown sugar
2 large eggs, at room
   temperature
1 teaspoon vanilla extract
16 tablespoons (2 sticks)
   unsalted butter, melted,
   cooled to tepid
½ cup unsweetened nonalkalized
   cocoa powder, such as
   Hershey's

¼ cup whole-wheat flour
¼ cup all-purpose flour
¼ teaspoon baking powder
¼ teaspoon salt
1 cup raisins

ICING
6 ounces European milk
   chocolate, finely chopped
1 cup raisins

1. *Brownie:* Position a rack in the center of the oven and preheat to 350°F. Lightly butter and flour a 9-inch square baking pan, tapping out excess flour.

2. In a medium bowl, whisk brown sugar, eggs, and vanilla until smooth. Whisk in melted butter. Using a wooden spoon, stir in cocoa, both flours, baking powder, and salt, just until blended. Stir in raisins.

3. Spread batter evenly into prepared pan and bake 25 to 30 minutes, until a toothpick inserted in the center comes out with a moist crumb. Cool completely on a wire cake rack.

4. *Icing:* In the top part of a double boiler, over hot, not simmering, water, melt milk chocolate, stirring often, until smooth. (Water should not be hotter than 125°F.) Stir in raisins and remove from heat. Using a metal cake spatula, spread icing evenly over top of brownie. Refrigerate 30 minutes to set icing.

MAKES 12 BROWNIES

# ZEBRA BROWNIES

These chewy two-tone treats combine the flavors of a butterscotch blondie studded with chocolate morsels and a rich, chocolaty brownie with white chocolate chips.

1 cup all-purpose flour	½ cup granulated sugar
1 teaspoon baking powder	½ cup packed light brown sugar
¼ teaspoon salt	1 large egg, lightly beaten
2 ounces semisweet chocolate, finely chopped	½ teaspoon vanilla extract
	½ cup white chocolate chips
8 tablespoons (1 stick) unsalted butter, cut into pieces	½ cup semisweet chocolate chips

1. Position a rack in the center of the oven and preheat to 350°F. Lightly butter and flour an 8-inch square baking pan, tapping out excess flour.

2. In a small bowl, sift together flour, baking powder, and salt. In the top of a double boiler, over hot, not simmering, water, melt chocolate. Off heat, let stand about 10 minutes, until tepid.

3. In a medium saucepan over low heat, melt butter. Off heat, whisk in both sugars until smooth, then cool for 5 minutes. Whisk in egg and vanilla. Using a wooden spoon, stir in flour mixture, just until blended.

4. Divide batter in half between two medium bowls. In one bowl, stir in the cooled chocolate and white chocolate chips. In the other bowl, stir in the semisweet chocolate chips. Spread half of the white batter in a 2″ × 8″ column in one-fourth of the prepared pan. (Batters are thick and will spread easily without running.) Spread half of the dark batter next to the white batter in a 2″ × 8″ column that fills another quarter of the pan. Repeat procedure with remaining batters, until you have four alternating rows of white and dark batters. Bake 18 to 22 minutes, until a toothpick inserted in the center comes out with a moist crumb. Cool completely on a wire cake rack. Cut into 16 black-and-white bars.

MAKES 16 BROWNIES

 # TROPICAL PARADISE BROWNIES

We've turned pineapple upside-down cake inside out and added a little chocolate and a dash of dark rum. Definitely for Adults Only!

3 ounces coarsely chopped dried pineapple (about ½ cup)
3 tablespoons dark rum, divided

½ cup all-purpose flour
2 tablespoons unsweetened nonalkalized cocoa powder, such as Hershey's
¼ teaspoon baking soda
¼ teaspoon salt

8 tablespoons (1 stick) unsalted butter, cut into pieces
2 ounces unsweetened chocolate, finely chopped
1 cup packed light brown sugar
2 large eggs
½ teaspoon vanilla
Confectioners' sugar, for garnish

1. In a small bowl, combine the dried pineapple and 2 tablespoons of the rum and let stand at least 1 hour, until the pineapple has absorbed most of the rum. Sift flour, cocoa, baking soda, and salt through a wire strainer onto a sheet of wax paper.

2. Position a rack in the center of the oven and preheat to 350°F. Lightly butter and flour an 8-inch square baking pan, tapping out excess flour.

3. In a medium saucepan over low heat, melt butter. Off heat, add chocolate and let stand 1 minute; whisk until smooth. Let stand 10 minutes, until tepid. Whisk in brown sugar. One at a time, whisk in eggs, then vanilla. Using a wooden spoon, stir in flour mixture, just until blended. Stir in rum-soaked pineapple chunks.

4. Spread batter evenly into prepared pan and bake 25 to 30 minutes, until a toothpick inserted in the center comes out with a moist crumb. Brush remaining tablespoon of rum over top of brownie. Cool completely on a wire cake rack. To garnish, sift confectioners' sugar through a wire strainer over top of brownie.

MAKES 12 BROWNIES

S'MORE BROWNIES

A wonderful picnic treat for kids of all ages. The classic graham-cracker-chocolate-marshmallow combination adds a delicious texture to this brownie favorite that will have the whole family clamoring for some more.

BOTTOM LAYER
¾ cup crushed graham cracker crumbs
3 tablespoons granulated sugar
3 tablespoons unsalted butter, melted

BROWNIE LAYER
8 tablespoons (1 stick) unsalted butter, cut into pieces
2 ounces unsweetened chocolate, finely chopped
1 cup granulated sugar
2 large eggs, at room temperature
½ teaspoon vanilla extract

½ cup all-purpose flour
⅛ teaspoon salt
3 ounces milk chocolate, finely chopped

TOPPING
1½ cups mini-marshmallows

1. *Bottom Layer:* Position a rack in the center of the oven and preheat to 350°F. Line an 8-inch square baking pan with a double thickness of aluminum foil so that the foil extends 2 inches beyond two opposite ends of the pan. Fold the overhang down to form "handles." Butter the bottom and sides of the foil-lined pan.

2. In a small bowl, mix graham cracker crumbs, sugar, and melted butter until combined. Press crumb mixture evenly into the bottom of the prepared pan.

3. *Brownie Layer:* In a medium saucepan over low heat, melt butter. Off heat, add chocolate and let stand 1 to 2 minutes; whisk until smooth. Whisk in sugar. One at a time, whisk in eggs, then add vanilla. Using a wooden spoon, stir in flour and salt, just until combined.

4. Spread brownie batter evenly over bottom crumb layer and bake 22 to 25 minutes, until a toothpick inserted in the center comes out with a moist crumb. *Do not overbake.* Sprinkle milk chocolate over top of warm brownie and let stand 5 minutes, until chocolate is melted. Using a metal cake spatula, spread chocolate evenly over top of brownie.

5. *Topping:* Position a broiler rack 5 to 6 inches from the source of heat and

preheat the broiler. While the brownie is still warm, sprinkle marshmallows evenly over the milk chocolate layer, covering the milk chocolate completely. Broil 20 to 30 seconds, or until golden brown. Cool completely on a wire cake rack. To cut, use a lightly oiled knife to prevent marshmallows from sticking. These brownies are best served right away.

MAKES 12 BROWNIES

11
ELEGANT AND EASY
BROWNIE DESSERTS

Easy to make, bake, and serve to family and guests. From a simple Valencia Brownie Torte to a Brownie Ice-Cream Sandwich, these desserts are designed to suit our hectic lifestyles and to offer indulgent rewards for making it through another crazy day. Try the Hot Mocha Mississippi Mud Brownie on a cold, wintry night or the Nirvana Brownie Truffles if you want to impress.

Nirvana Brownie Truffles
Chocolate Chip Blondie Pie
Brownie Ice-Cream Sandwiches
Chocolate Brownie Fruit Tart
Brownie Blackout Cake
Cappuccino Frozen Yogurt Brownie Pie
Teatime Brownie Loaf
Strawberries-and-Cream Brownie Shortcake
Ivory Brownie Dream Torte
Chocolate-Chocolate Brownie Chunk Cheesecake
Brownie Soufflé with Brandied Chocolate Sauce

Banana Cream Brownie Pie
Hot Mocha Mississippi Mud Brownie
Brownie Chunk Ice Cream
Steamed Brownie Pudding with Raspberry Sauce
Chocolate Brownie Bombe
Bittersweet Chocolate Mousse Squares
Valencia Brownie Torte
Layered Brownie Fudge Pudding Parfaits
Brownie-Chip Waffles
Chocolate-Dipped Brownie Fingers
Brownie Cookies

NIRVANA BROWNIE TRUFFLES

Fudgy in the center with slightly chewy edges. We love to pop a couple of these truffles straight from the freezer into our mouths. When entertaining, remove them from the freezer 5 minutes before serving. (Of course, they're certainly more than acceptable at room temperature, too.) Make a double batch, so you have a few on hand "just in case." Roll smaller truffle balls to use as fanciful cake decorations, or place them in miniature paper candy cups. Absolutely fabulous folded into our own Brownie Chunk Ice Cream (see Index), these truffles would enhance store-bought vanilla ice cream, too.

7 tablespoons unsalted butter, cut into pieces
6 ounces European bittersweet chocolate, finely chopped
½ cup granulated sugar
2 large eggs, at room temperature
1 teaspoon vanilla extract

⅓ cup all-purpose flour
1 tablespoon Grand Marnier
Grated zest of 1 medium orange
¼ teaspoon salt
½ cup unsweetened alkalized cocoa powder, such as Droste
¼ cup confectioners' sugar

1. Position a rack in the center of the oven and preheat to 350°F. Lightly butter an 8-inch square baking pan. Line the bottom of a baking sheet with wax paper.

2. In a medium saucepan over low heat, melt butter. Off heat, add chocolate and let stand 10 minutes; whisk until smooth. Whisk in sugar. One at a time, whisk in eggs, then vanilla. Using a wooden spoon, stir in flour, Grand Marnier, orange zest, and salt, just until blended.

3. Scrape batter evenly into prepared pan and bake 18 to 22 minutes, until a toothpick inserted 1 inch from the edge of the brownie comes out with a moist crumb. Center will be unset; *do not overbake.* Cool brownie on a wire cake rack for 45 minutes, until lukewarm. Using a tablespoon, scoop up a spoonful of the warm brownie and roll it between your hands to form a rough ball. Place it on the wax paper–lined baking sheet. Continue with the remaining brownie mixture, placing balls in a single layer on the prepared baking sheet. Freeze brownie truffles at least 2 hours, until firm. Brownie truffles will keep, tightly wrapped in aluminum foil and frozen, for up to 1 month.

4. Sift cocoa and confectioners' sugar into a small bowl. Up to 8 hours before serving, roll truffles in cocoa mixture to cover. Remove from freezer 5 minutes before serving.

MAKES ABOUT 24 BROWNIE TRUFFLES

# CHOCOLATE CHIP BLONDIE PIE

It's okay to cheat on this one—go ahead and slice it warm and enjoy the chewy butterscotch flavor accented with golden pecans and chocolate chips. A frosty scoop of vanilla ice cream provides a wonderful counterbalance to the rich, buttery pie.

1 cup all-purpose flour
¼ teaspoon baking soda
¼ teaspoon salt
8 tablespoons (1 stick) unsalted butter, at room temperature
1 cup packed light brown sugar
1 large egg, at room temperature

1 teaspoon vanilla extract
1 ounce pecan halves (about ¼ cup)
¼ cup semisweet chocolate chips (about 1½ ounces)
1 pint vanilla ice cream (optional)

1. Position a rack in the center of the oven and preheat to 350°F. Lightly butter a 9-inch round pie pan.

2. Sift flour, baking soda, and salt through a wire strainer into a medium bowl. In another medium bowl, using a hand-held electric mixer set at high speed, beat butter and brown sugar for 3 minutes, until light in color and texture. Beat in egg, then vanilla. Using a wooden spoon, stir in flour mixture, just until blended.

3. Spread batter evenly into prepared pan. Arrange pecan halves around the outside edge of the batter. Sprinkle chocolate chips in a single layer in the center of the pie. Bake 22 to 25 minutes, until a toothpick inserted in the center comes out with a moist crumb. Cool for about 30 minutes on a wire cake rack. To serve, cut into wedges while warm and accompany with a scoop of vanilla ice cream, if desired.

MAKES 8 SERVINGS

BROWNIE ICE-CREAM SANDWICHES

Ever get caught in the kitchen with dessert-demanding guests and nothing to serve? Keep a batch of these in the freezer and surprise the gang anytime.

BROWNIE LAYERS
12 tablespoons (1½ sticks) unsalted butter, cut into pieces
5 ounces unsweetened chocolate, finely chopped
6 large eggs, at room temperature
2 cups granulated sugar
2 tablespoons light corn syrup

2 teaspoons vanilla extract
1½ cups all-purpose flour
½ teaspoon salt
2 ounces walnuts, finely chopped (about ½ cup)

ICE-CREAM FILLING
3 pints ice cream (your favorite flavor), softened

1. *Brownie Layers:* Position a rack in the center of the oven and preheat to 350°F. Line an 11″ × 17″ jelly-roll pan with aluminum foil and lightly butter and flour foil, tapping out excess flour.

2. In a medium saucepan over low heat, melt butter. Off heat, add chocolate and let stand 1 minute; whisk until smooth. Let stand 10 minutes, until tepid.

3. In a medium bowl, using a hand-held electric mixer set at high speed, beat eggs and sugar for 2 to 3 minutes, until very light in color and texture. Beat in cooled chocolate mixture, corn syrup, and vanilla. Using a wooden spoon, stir in flour and salt, just until blended. Stir in walnuts.

4. Spread batter into prepared pan. Bake 12 to 15 minutes, just until a toothpick inserted in the center comes out with a moist crumb. Cool completely on a wire cake rack. Run a knife around inside edges of pan to release brownie from sides. Place a baking sheet on top of the brownie and invert. Carefully peel off foil. Cut brownie into two 11″ × 8½″ rectangles.

5. *Ice-Cream Filling:* Line an 11″ × 17″ jelly-roll pan with plastic wrap. Place

one rectangle, top crust up, on the plastic wrap. Using a metal cake spatula, spread ice cream evenly to cover brownie. Place the other brownie, top crust down, on ice cream. Wrap tightly in plastic wrap, pressing ice cream on sides to compact. Freeze overnight, until very firm.

6. Unwrap, and using a sharp knife, cut into 16 rectangles. Wrap each rectangle tightly in plastic wrap. Ice-cream sandwiches can be prepared up to 2 weeks ahead, wrapped tightly, and frozen.

MAKES 16 SANDWICHES

CHOCOLATE BROWNIE FRUIT TART

There are very few fruits that we don't love to combine with chocolate; however, bananas, raspberries, and strawberries are our favorites. Here they all are, crowning a chewy chocolate brownie base in a dessert that will remind you of a classic French fruit tart.

BROWNIE TART
6 tablespoons (¾ stick) unsalted butter, cut into pieces
3 ounces unsweetened chocolate, finely chopped
2 large eggs, at room temperature
1 cup packed light brown sugar
1 teaspoon vanilla extract
¼ teaspoon almond extract
½ cup all-purpose flour
¼ teaspoon baking soda
¼ teaspoon salt
2 ounces blanched almonds, finely chopped (about ½ cup)

FRESH-FRUIT TOPPING
½ cup apricot preserves
2 tablespoons water
2 ripe medium bananas, peeled, sliced ¼ inch thick
1 pint fresh raspberries
½ pint fresh strawberries, hulled

1. *Brownie Tart:* Position a rack in the center of the oven and preheat to 350°F.

Line the bottom of a 9-inch round cake pan with a wax-paper round; butter and flour sides of pan and tap out excess flour.

2. In a medium saucepan over low heat, melt butter. Off heat, add unsweetened chocolate and let stand 1 minute; whisk until smooth. Let stand for 10 minutes, until tepid.

3. In a medium bowl, using a hand-held electric mixer set at high speed, beat eggs and brown sugar for 2 to 3 minutes, until thick and light in color. Beat in chocolate mixture, then both extracts. Using a wooden spoon, stir in flour, baking soda, and salt, just until blended. Stir in almonds.

4. Spread batter evenly into prepared pan. Bake 20 to 25 minutes, until a toothpick inserted 1 inch from the edge of the brownie comes out clean. Cool on a wire cake rack for 10 minutes, then run a knife around the inside edge of the pan to release the brownie from the sides. Invert onto a wire cake rack, carefully peel off wax paper, and cool completely.

5. *Fresh-Fruit Topping:* In a small saucepan over medium heat, bring preserves and water to a simmer; cook 2 minutes. Strain apricot mixture through a wire strainer into a small bowl.

6. Arrange bananas, overlapping, in a circle around outside edge of brownie round. Arrange raspberries, rounded sides up, in circle inside banana circle. Arrange strawberries, hulled sides down, in center of brownie round. Brush warm apricot mixture over fruit. Brownie can be made up to 3 days ahead, wrapped tightly, and refrigerated. Brownie with fruit topping may be prepared and refrigerated up to 8 hours before serving. Remove from refrigerator 30 minutes before serving.

MAKES 8 TO 10 SERVINGS

BROWNIE BLACKOUT CAKE

Deep, dark, decadent. The rich, fudgy goodness of a brownie mated with a moist, high-rise chocolate cake—a heavenly delicious marriage.

FILLING
½ cup semisweet chocolate chips (about 3 ounces)
2 ounces walnuts, coarsely chopped (about ½ cup)
¼ cup packed light brown sugar
1 tablespoon unsweetened non-alkalized cocoa powder, such as Hershey's

BLACKOUT CAKE
2½ cups all-purpose flour
½ cup unsweetened nonalkalized cocoa powder, such as Hershey's
1½ teaspoons baking powder
1 teaspoon baking soda
½ teaspoon salt
12 tablespoons (1½ sticks) unsalted butter, at room temperature
1 cup granulated sugar
½ cup packed light brown sugar
3 large eggs, at room temperature
1 teaspoon vanilla extract
2 cups sour cream, at room temperature

GLAZE
¼ cup heavy cream
4 ounces bittersweet or semisweet chocolate, finely chopped
1 teaspoon instant coffee powder dissolved in 1 tablespoon boiling water
1 ounce walnuts, finely chopped (about ¼ cup)

1. *Filling:* In a small bowl, combine chocolate chips, walnuts, brown sugar, and cocoa with fingers until well mixed.

2. *Blackout Cake:* Position a rack in the center of the oven and preheat to 350°F. Generously butter the inside of a 10- to 12-cup fluted tube pan. Lightly dust the inside of the pan with flour, tapping out excess flour. Sift flour, cocoa, baking powder, baking soda, and salt through a wire strainer onto a piece of wax paper.

3. In a large bowl, using a hand-held electric mixer set at high speed, beat butter 1 minute, until creamy. Gradually add both sugars and continue beating for 2 minutes, until light in texture and color. One at a time, beat in eggs, then vanilla. One-third at a time, alternately add flour mixture and sour cream, beating well after each addition, and scraping down sides of bowl as necessary.

4. Spoon one-third of the batter into prepared pan. Sprinkle half of the filling over the batter. Spoon another third of the batter over the filling. Top with remaining filling. Spoon remaining batter over filling, covering filling completely and smoothing the top with a rubber spatula. Bake 55 minutes to 1 hour, until a toothpick inserted in the center of the cake comes out clean. Cool for 10 minutes on a wire cake rack, then invert onto the cake rack and remove tube pan. Cool completely before glazing.

5. *Glaze:* In a small saucepan over low heat, bring cream to a low simmer. Off heat, add chocolate and dissolved coffee and let stand for 1 minute; whisk until smooth. Transfer to a small bowl and let stand about 10 minutes, until tepid. Place a large piece of wax paper underneath the cake on the wire cake rack and pour glaze over top of cake, letting excess run down sides. Sprinkle top of cake with chopped walnuts. Refrigerate cake for 15 minutes to set glaze. Cake can be made up to 1 day in advance, covered with plastic wrap, and stored at room temperature.

MAKES 10 TO 12 SERVINGS

CAPPUCCINO FROZEN YOGURT BROWNIE PIE

Although we consider ourselves devout ice-cream fanatics, we occasionally crave a lighter, yet equally satisfying, alternative. Coffee frozen yogurt, touched with cinnamon, is smoothed into a brownie crust, with a ribbon of thick fudge sauce in between and a drizzle of extra hot fudge on top.

FUDGY BROWNIE CRUST
8 tablespoons (1 stick) unsalted butter, cut into pieces
3 ounces unsweetened chocolate, finely chopped
1 cup packed light brown sugar
2 large eggs, at room temperature
2 teaspoons vanilla extract
⅔ cup all-purpose flour
¼ teaspoon ground cinnamon
¼ teaspoon salt

HOT-FUDGE SAUCE
1½ cups granulated sugar
1 cup plus 2 tablespoons unsweetened cocoa, sifted
1½ cups heavy cream
3 tablespoons light corn syrup
6 tablespoons (¾ stick) unsalted butter, cut into pieces

FILLING
4 pints coffee-flavored frozen yogurt, slightly softened
¼ teaspoon ground cinnamon

1. *Brownie Crust:* Position a rack in the center of the oven and preheat to 350°F. Lightly oil a 9-inch round pie pan.

2. In a medium saucepan over low heat, melt butter. Off heat, add chocolate and let stand 1 minute; whisk until smooth. Let stand 10 minutes, until tepid. Whisk in brown sugar. One at a time, whisk in eggs, then vanilla. Using a wooden spoon, stir in flour, cinnamon, and salt, just until blended.

3. Spread batter evenly into prepared pan and bake 18 to 22 minutes, until a toothpick inserted in the center comes out with a moist crumb. Cool for 30 minutes on a wire cake rack. Protecting your hands with a folded piece of wax paper, press the partially cooled brownie down and up along the sides of the pan to make a crust of even thickness. Cool completely on the wire cake rack.

4. *Hot-Fudge Sauce:* Prepare fudge sauce just before filling brownie crust with frozen yogurt: In a heavy-bottomed medium saucepan, whisk together sugar and cocoa to combine. Gradually whisk in cream to dissolve cocoa. Whisk in corn syrup and butter. Bring to a simmer over medium heat, stirring constantly with a wooden spoon. Reduce heat to low, and simmer, without stirring, for 5 to 6 minutes, until slightly thickened. Remove from heat. Reserve ¾ cup of fudge sauce and keep warm. Cover remaining fudge sauce with plastic wrap and refrigerate until ready to serve.

5. *Filling:* In a large bowl, using a wooden spoon, combine softened coffee frozen yogurt and cinnamon. Spread one-third of the frozen yogurt evenly over the cooled crust. Drizzle reserved ¾ cup of fudge sauce over the top of the frozen yogurt. (Sauce will harden when it touches the cold frozen yogurt.) Using a large rubber spatula, mound remaining frozen yogurt on top of fudge layer, and smooth frozen yogurt into a high dome. Cover pie with plastic wrap and freeze overnight, until firm.

6. When ready to serve, transfer frozen yogurt pie in pan to a large plate and refrigerate for 15 to 30 minutes, until slightly softened. Reheat remaining fudge sauce in the top part of a double boiler over hot, not simmering, water, stirring often, until smooth. Rinse a sharp knife under hot water and wipe dry. Using the hot knife, cut pie into wedges. Serve each wedge with a drizzle of hot-fudge sauce.

MAKES 8 TO 10 SERVINGS

TEATIME BROWNIE LOAF

When you want something chocolaty, but not too sweet, try a slice of this light-textured nutty chocolate bread. This brownie loaf is also a wonderful made-ahead dessert—simply slice and serve.

2 cups plus 2 tablespoons all-purpose flour, divided
¾ cup unsweetened nonalkalized cocoa powder, such as Hershey's
1 teaspoon salt
½ teaspoon baking soda
1½ cups (3 sticks) unsalted butter, at room temperature

2 cups granulated sugar
1 cup packed light brown sugar
5 large eggs, at room temperature
2 teaspoons vanilla extract
1 teaspoon instant espresso powder dissolved in ¼ cup boiling water

1 cup milk, at room temperature
2 ounces walnuts, finely chopped (about ½ cup)
½ cup semisweet chocolate chips (about 3 ounces)

1. Position a rack in the center of the oven and preheat to 350°F. Lightly butter and flour two 8½″ × 4½″ loaf pans, tapping out excess flour.

2. Sift 2 cups of flour, cocoa, salt, and baking soda through a wire strainer onto a piece of wax paper. In a large bowl, using a hand-held electric mixer set at high speed, beat butter for 1 minute, until creamy. Gradually add both sugars and continue beating for 2 minutes, until very light in color and texture. One at a time, beat in eggs, beating well after each addition. Beat in vanilla. Stir dissolved coffee into milk. Alternately beat in flour mixture and milk mixture, just until blended. In a small bowl, toss walnuts and chips to coat with remaining 2 tablespoons of flour, and stir into batter.

3. Divide batter evenly between prepared pans and smooth tops. Bake 40 to 45 minutes, until a toothpick inserted in the centers of the tea loaves comes out clean. Cool completely on a wire cake rack.

MAKES 2 LOAVES

STRAWBERRIES-AND-CREAM BROWNIE SHORTCAKE

Picnic-perfect, this light and airy strawberry shortcake features Grand Marnier-doused sliced strawberries and freshly whipped cream sandwiched between two brownie cake layers.

BROWNIE
1¼ cups granulated sugar
½ cup unsweetened nonalkalized cocoa powder, such as Hershey's
¼ teaspoon baking soda
⅛ teaspoon salt
¼ cup boiling water
8 tablespoons (1 stick) unsalted butter, melted
½ cup all-purpose flour
¼ cup sour cream, at room temperature
1 large egg, at room temperature, lightly beaten
¼ teaspoon vanilla extract

FILLING
1 pint fresh strawberries, hulled and sliced
3 tablespoons granulated sugar, or to taste
2 tablespoons Grand Marnier (optional)

TOPPING
1 cup heavy cream
2 tablespoons confectioners' sugar
1 tablespoon Grand Marnier (optional)

1. *Brownie:* Position a rack in the center of the oven and preheat to 350°F. Lightly butter and flour an 8-inch round cake pan, tapping out excess flour.

2. Sift sugar, cocoa, baking soda, and salt into a medium mixing bowl. Whisk in boiling water and melted butter until smooth. Using a wooden spoon, stir in flour, sour cream, egg, and vanilla, just until smooth.

3. Spread batter evenly into prepared pan and bake 25 to 30 minutes, until a toothpick inserted in the center comes out clean. Cool completely on a wire cake rack.

4. *Filling:* In a medium bowl, combine strawberries, sugar, and Grand Marnier, if desired. Cover with plastic wrap and refrigerate at least 2 hours, until strawberries release their juice.

5. *Topping:* Just before serving, in a chilled medium bowl, using a hand-held electric mixer set at high speed, beat heavy cream and confectioners' sugar just until soft peaks begin to form. Beat in Grand Marnier, if desired, just until blended.

6. Using a long serrated knife, slice cooled brownie in half horizontally. Slide a flat plate or an 8-inch cardboard round under the top half of the brownie to support it, and set top half aside. Place strawberries on bottom half of brownie, and top with about half of the sweetened whipped cream. Place top half of brownie on sweetened whipped cream. Slice into eight pieces and serve immediately, with a dollop of the remaining whipped cream on the side.

MAKES 8 SERVINGS

IVORY BROWNIE DREAM TORTE

A rich, buttery, vanilla-scented white-chocolate-chunk brownie pie with toasted cashews. Additional cashew pieces are pressed into an ivory frosting on the sides of the torte.

WHITE CHOCOLATE BROWNIE

6 tablespoons (¾ stick) unsalted butter, cut into pieces

3 ounces white chocolate, finely chopped

2 large eggs, at room temperature

1 cup packed light brown sugar

1 teaspoon vanilla extract

1¼ cups all-purpose flour

½ teaspoon baking powder

¼ teaspoon salt

3 ounces white chocolate, coarsely chopped

2 ounces cashews, rinsed of salt, patted dry, and coarsely chopped (about ½ cup)

FROSTING

¼ cup heavy cream

3 ounces white chocolate, chopped fine

4 ounces cashews, rinsed of salt, patted dry, and coarsely chopped (about 1 cup)

1 tablespoon confectioners' sugar, for dusting

1. *Brownie:* Position a rack in the center of the oven and preheat to 350° F. Line the bottom of a 9-inch round cake pan with a wax-paper round; lightly butter and flour the sides of the pan, tapping out excess flour.

2. In the top part of a double boiler over hot, not simmering, water, melt butter. (Water should be no warmer than 125° F.) Add half of the white chocolate and let stand 1 minute; whisk until almost smooth. Add remaining white chocolate and melt, whisking often until smooth. Transfer to a medium bowl and let stand 10 minutes, until tepid.

3. In a medium bowl, using a hand-held electric mixer set at high speed, beat eggs and brown sugar for 2 to 3 minutes, until thick and light in color. Beat in cooled white chocolate, then vanilla. Using a wooden spoon, stir in flour, baking powder, and salt. Stir in white chocolate chunks and cashews.

4. Spread batter evenly into prepared pan and bake 25 to 30 minutes, until a toothpick inserted in the center comes out with a moist crumb. Cool on a wire cake rack for 10 minutes, then run a sharp knife around the inside edge of the pan to release the brownie from the sides. Invert onto the wire cake rack, carefully peel off wax paper, and cool completely.

5. *Frosting:* In a small saucepan over low heat, bring cream to a simmer. Off heat, add white chocolate and let stand 1 to 2 minutes; whisk until smooth. Transfer to a small bowl, and refrigerate for about 45 minutes, until thick enough to spread. Using a metal cake spatula, spread frosting on sides of brownie. Press chopped cashews onto sides of torte. Refrigerate torte for 30 minutes to set frosting. Torte can be covered with plastic wrap and refrigerated up to 2 days ahead. To serve, sift confectioners' sugar through a wire strainer over top of cake. Serve at room temperature.

MAKES 8 TO 10 SERVINGS

CHOCOLATE-CHOCOLATE BROWNIE CHUNK CHEESECAKE

The inspiration for this recipe came from Maida Heatter, the doyenne of desserts, whom we believe created the first brownie cheesecake. Dedicated to serious chocophiles, our version features a deep, dark, chocolate cheesecake with brownie chunks in a chocolate cookie crust.

BROWNIE CHUNKS
½ batch Traditional Fudgy or Classic Chewy Brownies (see Index and Note) **or** ½ batch of your favorite recipe

COOKIE CRUST
¾ cup crushed chocolate wafer cookies (about 3½ ounces)
2 tablespoons granulated sugar
2 tablespoons unsalted butter, melted

CHOCOLATE CHEESECAKE
6 ounces semisweet chocolate, coarsely chopped
24 ounces (3 8-ounce packages) cream cheese, at room temperature
1 cup granulated sugar
2 large eggs, at room temperature
¼ cup sour cream, at room temperature
1 tablespoon cornstarch
1 teaspoon vanilla extract

Chocolate Leaves (see Index) for garnish (optional)

1. *Brownie Chunks:* Cut brownies into ½-inch cubes.

2. *Cookie Crust:* Position a rack in the center of the oven and preheat to 325°F. Lightly butter a 9½-inch round springform pan. Wrap a double thickness of aluminum foil around the outside of the pan.

3. In a small bowl, mix cookie crumbs, sugar, and melted butter until well combined. Press mixture firmly and evenly onto the bottom and one-fourth up the sides of the prepared pan.

4. *Chocolate Cheesecake:* In the top part of a double boiler, over hot, not simmering, water, melt chocolate. Remove from heat and let stand 10 minutes, until tepid.

5. In a medium bowl, using a hand-held electric mixer set at high speed, beat cream cheese and sugar for 2 minutes, until very smooth. One at a time, add eggs, beating well after each addition. Beat in melted chocolate, sour cream, cornstarch, and vanilla, scraping the sides of the bowl with a rubber spatula as necessary, until well mixed. Using a wooden spoon, fold in brownie chunks. Scrape batter evenly into prepared pan.

6. Place the springform pan in a larger baking pan and pour enough hot water into the larger pan to come halfway up the sides of the springform pan. Bake 50 minutes to 1 hour, until the edges of the cake have risen slightly and are beginning to brown. Remove the springform pan from the water, run a sharp knife around the inside edge of the pan to release the cake from the sides, and cool completely on a wire cake rack. Remove the sides of the springform pan. Refrigerate, covered with plastic wrap, at least 4 hours, or overnight. Just before serving, garnish cheesecake with chocolate leaves. The cheesecake will keep, covered tightly with plastic wrap and refrigerated, for up to 3 days.

MAKES 12 TO 16 SERVINGS

Note: Eat the other half of the batch, share with friends, or save for another use. Brownie Chunk Ice Cream and Layered Brownie Fudge Pudding Parfaits (see Index) also use ½ batch of Traditional Fudgy or Classic Chewy Brownies. Freeze leftover brownies until ready to use.

BROWNIE SOUFFLE WITH BRANDIED CHOCOLATE SAUCE

A brownie that rises to any occasion in grand, light style. Lightly beaten egg whites are folded into a brownie-style batter and baked into a delicate chocolate puff. During baking, the air trapped in the egg whites expands and increases the volume of the soufflé, so don't open the oven door! A brandy-laced chocolate sauce accompanies this lovely dessert.

CHOCOLATE SAUCE
⅓ cup heavy cream
6 ounces bittersweet or
   semisweet chocolate,
   finely chopped
1 tablespoon brandy or Cognac
¼ teaspoon vanilla extract
1 ounce walnuts, toasted, finely
   chopped (about ¼ cup)

SOUFFLE
½ cup packed light brown sugar
2 tablespoons cornstarch
1 cup milk
2 ounces semisweet chocolate,
   finely chopped
3 large eggs, separated, plus
   2 additional large egg whites,
   at room temperature
½ teaspoon vanilla extract
Pinch salt

1. *Sauce:* In a medium saucepan over low heat, bring cream to a low simmer. Off heat, add chocolate and let stand 1 minute; whisk until smooth. Whisk in brandy and vanilla, then stir in nuts. Sauce can be made up to 3 days ahead, covered, and refrigerated. Reheat gently over very low heat, stirring constantly.

2. *Soufflé:* Position a rack in the center of the oven and preheat to 375°F. Wrap a long sheet of aluminum foil around the outside of a 1½-quart soufflé dish, forming a collar that rises 2 inches above the dish. Butter the inside of the soufflé dish and the foil, and dust with granulated sugar, tapping out excess sugar.

3. In a heavy-bottomed, medium saucepan, combine brown sugar and cornstarch. Add about ¼ cup of milk, and whisk until dissolved. Add remaining milk and bring to a simmer over medium heat, whisking constantly, about 2 minutes. Reduce heat to very low and cook for 2 minutes. Remove from heat and whisk in chopped chocolate. Whisk in egg yolks, then vanilla. Transfer mixture to a large bowl.

4. In a large, grease-free bowl, using a hand-held electric mixer set at medium speed, beat all 5 egg whites until foamy. Add salt, increase speed to high, and continue beating just until stiff peaks begin to form. Stir one-fourth of the egg whites into the chocolate mixture to lighten it. Fold in remaining whites.

5. Carefully pour batter into the prepared soufflé dish. Place soufflé dish in larger baking dish and place in oven. Quickly pour enough hot water into baking dish to rise 1 inch up sides of soufflé dish. Bake 35 to 45 minutes, until soufflé is puffed and a long cake tester inserted in the center of the soufflé comes out with a moist crumb. (The shorter baking time will give you a moister, less cakelike soufflé.) Serve immediately with warm chocolate sauce.

MAKES 4 TO 6 SERVINGS

 BANANA CREAM BROWNIE PIE

An all-American dream pie, with sliced bananas and a pudding custard piled on a brownie bottom, this is one of our favorite "comfort desserts." The brownie crust is inspired by a technique originated by food writer Betty Rosbottom.

BROWNIE CRUST
8 tablespoons (1 stick) unsalted butter, cut into pieces
2½ ounces unsweetened chocolate, finely chopped
1 cup plus 2 tablespoons granulated sugar
2 large eggs, at room temperature
½ teaspoon vanilla extract
⅔ cup all-purpose flour
¼ teaspoon salt
2 ounces walnuts, finely chopped (about ½ cup)

BANANA FILLING
3 large egg yolks
½ cup granulated sugar
5 teaspoons cornstarch
¼ teaspoon salt
1½ cups milk
2 tablespoons unsalted butter
1 teaspoon vanilla extract
3 ripe medium bananas, peeled, sliced ½-inch thick

TOPPING
1 cup heavy cream
2 tablespoons confectioners' sugar
¼ teaspoon vanilla extract
Chocolate curls, for garnish (see Index)

1. *Brownie Crust:* Position a rack in the center of the oven and preheat to 350°F. Lightly butter a 9-inch round pie pan.

2. In a medium saucepan over low heat, melt butter. Off heat, add chocolate and let stand 1 minute; whisk until smooth. Let stand 10 minutes, until tepid. Whisk in sugar. One at a time, whisk in eggs, then vanilla. Whisk in cooled chocolate mixture. Using a wooden spoon, stir in flour and salt, just until blended. Stir in chopped walnuts.

3. Spread batter evenly in bottom of prepared pie pan and bake 18 to 22 minutes, until a toothpick inserted 1 inch from the edge of the brownie comes out with a moist crumb. Cool on a wire cake rack for 30 minutes, until lukewarm. Protecting your hands with a folded piece of wax paper, press the warm brownie down and up onto the sides of the pan, until you have a brownie-crust shell of even thickness. Cool brownie crust completely.

4. *Filling:* In a heavy-bottomed medium saucepan, whisk together egg yolks, sugar, cornstarch, and salt. Gradually whisk in cold milk. Add butter and bring to a simmer over medium heat, stirring constantly with a wooden spoon. Reduce heat to low and simmer, stirring constantly, for 5 minutes. Off heat, stir in vanilla. Transfer to a medium bowl. Place a piece of plastic wrap directly onto surface of filling and pierce wrap with a sharp knife in several places to allow steam to escape. Refrigerate for at least 2 hours, until cool and set.

5. *Topping:* In a chilled medium bowl, using a hand-held electric mixer set at high speed, beat cream, confectioners' sugar, and vanilla until soft peaks begin to form.

6. Arrange banana slices on bottom of cooled brownie crust. Spread filling evenly over bananas. Using a metal cake spatula, swirl whipped-cream topping over filling. To garnish, sprinkle top of whipped cream with chocolate curls. Pie can be prepared up to 1 day ahead and refrigerated, uncovered, until ready to serve.

MAKES 8 SERVINGS

HOT MOCHA MISSISSIPPI MUD BROWNIE

Rick remembers a recipe like this as his childhood favorite. But, with the addition of coffee, it becomes slightly more grownup than before. We tried many, many "Mississippi Mud" variations. This final one, our favorite, uses very basic ingredients, which, when baked, transform themselves into the two best parts of a brownie: warm baked chocolate crust and hot fudgy mocha sauce.

1 cup all-purpose flour
1¾ cups packed light brown sugar, divided
¼ cup plus 3 tablespoons unsweetened nonalkalized cocoa powder, such as Hershey's, divided

2 teaspoons baking powder
¼ teaspoon salt
½ cup milk
2 tablespoons unsalted butter, melted
½ teaspoon vanilla extract

2 ounces walnuts, coarsely chopped (about ½ cup)
1¾ cups hot brewed coffee
1 quart vanilla ice cream (optional)

1. Position a rack in the center of the oven and preheat to 350°F.

2. Sift flour, 1 cup brown sugar, 3 tablespoons cocoa, baking powder, and salt through a wire strainer into a medium bowl, rubbing the brown sugar through. Stir in milk, melted butter, and vanilla, just until smooth. Stir in walnuts. Spread into an ungreased 9-inch square baking pan.

3. In a small bowl, combine the remaining ¾ cup brown sugar and remaining ¼ cup cocoa powder and sprinkle brown sugar/cocoa mixture over top of batter. Pour hot coffee over brown sugar/cocoa mixture.

4. Bake 40 to 45 minutes, until a toothpick inserted halfway down into the center of the baked brownie top comes out clean. Spoon the baked brownie top and hot mocha sauce that has formed into bowls and serve immediately. Top with vanilla ice cream, if desired.

MAKES 6 TO 8 SERVINGS

 # BROWNIE CHUNK ICE CREAM

A surprisingly light, but creamy, French custard-style chocolate ice cream with bite-size brownie chunks. Nirvana Brownie Truffles (see Index) are highly recommended for the chunks here, but Traditional Fudgy or Classic Chewy Brownies (see Index), or even trimmings from St. Valentine's Brownie Hearts (see Index) are all perfect additions. This recipe requires an ice-cream maker.

BROWNIE CHUNKS	CHOCOLATE ICE CREAM
½ batch Nirvana Brownie Truffles, Traditional Fudgy or Classic Chewy Brownies, or St. Valentine's Strawberry Brownie Hearts (see Note)	6 large egg yolks
	¾ cup granulated sugar
	3 tablespoons unsweetened cocoa powder
	3 cups half-and-half
	6 ounces semisweet chocolate, finely chopped

1. *Brownie Chunks:* Cut brownies into ½-inch cubes.

2. *Chocolate Ice Cream:* In a medium bowl, whisk together egg yolks, sugar, and cocoa until well mixed. In a medium, heavy, nonaluminum saucepan over medium-low heat, bring half-and-half to a simmer. Whisk about 1 cup of hot half-and-half into egg-yolk mixture until well blended. Gradually stir this mixture back into the saucepan. Continue cooking over medium-low heat, stirring constantly with a wooden spoon, until custard has thickened enough to coat the back of the spoon. *Do not let the custard boil.* Strain mixture through a wire strainer into a medium bowl. Add chopped chocolate, let stand for 1 minute, then whisk until smooth. Place the bowl in a larger bowl filled with iced water, and stir mixture occasionally for 15 to 20 minutes, until cold. Place a medium stainless-steel bowl in the freezer.

3. Pour mixture into the container of an ice-cream maker and freeze according to the manufacturer's directions. Remove the container from the machine. Transfer ice cream to the frozen bowl, then stir in the brownie chunks. Cover tightly with plastic wrap, then aluminum foil, and freeze for at least 4 hours, until solid.

4. Divide ice cream between chilled dessert bowls and serve immediately.

MAKES 6 TO 8 ½-CUP SERVINGS

Note: Eat the other half of the batch, share with friends, or freeze and save for another use. Chocolate-Chocolate Brownie Chunk Cheesecake and Layered Brownie Fudge Pudding Parfaits (see Index) also use ½ batch of brownies.

STEAMED BROWNIE PUDDING WITH RASPBERRY SAUCE

Here's a brownie dessert generally reserved for holidays that we enjoy year-round. Fashioned after an English steamed pudding, it is firm enough to be sliced, whereas our American puddings are spooned. Served warm, it has a flavor similar to our favorite hot chocolate, but in cake form.

STEAMED BROWNIE PUDDING

6 ounces semisweet chocolate, coarsely chopped

6 large eggs, separated, at room temperature

1 cup granulated sugar

½ teaspoon vanilla extract

¼ cup plus 1 tablespoon all-purpose flour, divided

½ teaspoon baking powder

½ teaspoon baking soda

4 ounces (about ½ cup) pecans, coarsely chopped

¼ teaspoon salt

RASPBERRY SAUCE

2 cups fresh or frozen, defrosted raspberries

¼ cup superfine sugar, or to taste (see Note)

3 tablespoons raspberry liqueur, such as Framboise (optional)

2 teaspoons fresh lemon juice, or to taste

1. *Steamed Pudding:* Generously butter the inside of an 8-cup steamed pudding mold or Bundt pan. Dust the inside with granulated sugar, tapping out excess sugar. Generously butter the inside of the mold's lid.

2. In the top of a double boiler, over hot, not simmering, water, melt chocolate. Remove from heat and let stand about 10 minutes, until tepid.

3. In a large bowl, using a hand-held electric mixer set at high speed, beat egg yolks and sugar about 3 minutes, until mixture is pale yellow and forms a thick ribbon when the beaters are lifted. Beat in cooled chocolate and vanilla. Beat in flour, baking powder, and baking soda, just until mixed. Stir in pecans.

4. Using a hand-held electric mixer with clean, dry beaters, set at low speed, beat egg whites in a grease-free medium bowl until they start to foam. Add salt, gradually increase speed to high, and continue beating until egg whites begin to form stiff peaks. Stir one-fourth of the whites into the chocolate mixture to lighten, then carefully fold in the remaining whites. Pour batter into prepared pan. Place lid on mold. (If your mold does not have a lid, or if you are using a Bundt pan, cover the top tightly with a double layer of buttered aluminum foil.)

5. Place covered mold in a large pot. Add enough boiling water to come halfway up the sides of the mold. Cover pot tightly and bring to a boil over high heat. Reduce heat to low and steam the pudding, keeping water at a simmer at all times and adding more boiling water as necessary, until a toothpick inserted in the center of the pudding comes out clean—about 1 hour and 45 minutes. Transfer pudding to a wire cake rack and cool for 5 minutes.

6. *Raspberry Sauce:* In a blender or food processor fitted with the metal chopping blade, puree raspberries, superfine sugar, liqueur (if desired), and lemon juice until smooth. Using a wooden spoon, strain and rub the sauce through a wire strainer into a medium bowl, discarding the seeds.

7. Slice pudding into wedges and serve warm, with raspberry sauce.

Note: You can make your own superfine sugar by processing granulated sugar in a blender or a food processor fitted with the metal blade until very finely ground.

MAKES 8 TO 10 SERVINGS

CHOCOLATE BROWNIE BOMBE

Three types of ice cream are piled high in a dome shape on a fudgy brownie crust. These are our favorite ice-cream flavors, but feel free to substitute your own. You will want to use the accompanying no-fail chocolate sauce with other recipes, too.

BROWNIE CRUST
8 tablespoons (1 stick) unsalted butter, cut into pieces
2 ounces unsweetened chocolate, finely chopped
1 cup granulated sugar
2 large eggs, at room temperature
1 teaspoon vanilla extract
½ cup all-purpose flour
¼ teaspoon salt

ICE-CREAM FILLING
½ gallon cookies 'n' cream ice cream
1 quart mocha-almond-fudge ice cream
1 pint chocolate-chocolate chip ice cream, slightly softened

NO-FAIL CHOCOLATE SAUCE
1 cup heavy cream
2 tablespoons unsalted butter
4 ounces bittersweet chocolate, finely chopped
1 ounce unsweetened chocolate, finely chopped

WHIPPED-CREAM TOPPING
2 cups heavy cream
¼ cup confectioners' sugar

Chocolate curls, for garnish (see Index)

1. *Brownie Crust:* Position a rack in the center of the oven and preheat to 350°F. Lightly butter and flour a 10-inch round baking pan, tapping out excess flour.

2. In a medium saucepan over low heat, melt butter. Off heat, add chocolate and let stand 1 minute; whisk until smooth. Let stand 10 minutes, until tepid. Whisk in sugar. One at a time, whisk in eggs, then vanilla. Using a wooden spoon, stir in flour and salt, just until blended.

3. Spread batter evenly into prepared pan and bake 12 to 15 minutes, until a toothpick inserted 1 inch from the edge of the brownie comes out with a moist crumb. Cool completely on a wire cake rack. Brownie can be made up to 2 days ahead, wrapped tightly in plastic wrap, and stored at room temperature.

4. *Ice-Cream Filling:* Line a 10-inch-diameter metal bowl with foil, allowing 2 inches of foil to hang over edge of bowl. Freeze bowl for 5 minutes.

5. Rinse a sharp knife under hot water and wipe dry. Using the hot knife, slice cookies 'n' cream ice cream into six slices. Arrange five slices, overlapping slightly, around inside of bowl. Cut remaining slice into pieces to fill any bare spots. Quickly press slices together to form a solid wall of ice cream. Freeze bowl for 5 minutes. Using the hot knife, slice mocha-almond ice cream into four slices, and quickly press them against cookies 'n' cream ice cream to make another layer. Freeze bowl for 5 minutes. Fill empty space in center of bowl with chocolate-chocolate chip ice cream. Smooth top of ice cream and cover with additional foil. Freeze for at least 4 hours, or overnight.

6. *Chocolate Sauce:* In a medium saucepan over low heat, bring cream and butter to a slow simmer, stirring to melt butter. Off heat, add both chocolates and let stand 1 minute; whisk until smooth. Serve chocolate sauce warm. Sauce can be made up to 2 days ahead, covered, and refrigerated. Reheat gently in top of a double boiler over hot, not simmering, water.

7. *Topping:* Just before serving, in a chilled medium bowl, using a hand-held electric mixer set at high speed, beat cream and confectioners' sugar just until soft peaks begin to form.

8. Remove top covering of aluminum foil from ice-cream bombe. Run a sharp knife around inside edges of baking pan to release brownie, and invert onto top of bombe. Place a 12-inch round serving plate on top of brownie and invert. Remove bowl, then carefully peel away aluminum foil. Using a metal cake spatula, frost the bombe with whipped cream. Garnish with chocolate curls, if desired. Cut bombe into wedges, then serve immediately with warm chocolate sauce.

MAKES 10 TO 12 SERVINGS

# BITTERSWEET CHOCOLATE
MOUSSE SQUARES

Opposites attract—in this case a dark, dense, fudgy brownie square with a light, airy froth of bittersweet chocolate mousse on top.

BROWNIE
6 tablespoons (¾ stick) unsalted
   butter, cut into pieces
1 ounce unsweetened chocolate
½ cup granulated sugar
1 large egg, at room
   temperature
¼ teaspoon vanilla extract
⅓ cup all-purpose flour
⅛ teaspoon baking soda
⅛ teaspoon salt

BITTERSWEET MOUSSE
4 ounces bittersweet chocolate,
   finely chopped
3 tablespoons strong brewed
   coffee
3 large eggs, separated, at room
   temperature
¾ cup heavy cream

TOPPING
⅓ cup heavy cream
1 tablespoon confectioners'
   sugar
6 to 9 chocolate espresso beans,
   for garnish

1. *Brownie:* Position a rack in the center of the oven and preheat to 350°F. Line an 8-inch square baking pan with a double thickness of aluminum foil so that the foil extends beyond the two opposite ends of the pan. Fold the overhang down to form "handles." Lightly butter the bottom and sides of the foil-lined pan.

2. In a medium saucepan over low heat, melt butter. Off heat, add unsweetened chocolate and let stand 1 minute; whisk until smooth. Let stand 10 minutes, until tepid. Whisk in sugar. Whisk in egg, then vanilla. Using a wooden spoon, stir in flour, baking soda, and salt, just until smooth.

3. Spread batter evenly into prepared pan and bake 10 to 12 minutes, just until a toothpick inserted in the center comes out with a moist crumb. *Do not overbake.* Cool completely on a wire cake rack.

4. *Mousse:* In the top part of a double boiler, over hot, not simmering, water,

melt the bittersweet chocolate with the coffee, stirring often until smooth. One at a time, whisk in egg yolks; remove from heat.

5. In a chilled medium bowl, using a hand-held electric mixer set at medium-high speed, beat heavy cream just until soft peaks form. In a grease-free bowl, using a hand-held electric mixer with clean beaters, set at medium-high speed, beat egg whites just until soft peaks begin to form. Stir one-fourth of the beaten whites into the chocolate-coffee mixture to lighten. Carefully fold in remaining whites. Gently fold in whipped cream. Using a metal cake spatula, spread chocolate mousse evenly over top of cooled brownie. Cover tightly with plastic wrap and refrigerate 4 hours or overnight, until mousse is firm.

6. *Topping:* In a chilled medium bowl, using a hand-held electric mixer set at medium-high speed, beat heavy cream and confectioners' sugar until soft peaks begin to form. Transfer whipped cream to a pastry bag fitted with a large star tube.

7. Run a knife around the inside edges of the pan to release mousse and brownie from sides. Lift up on "handles" to remove brownie from pan. Cut the brownie into six rectangles or nine squares and transfer to a serving dish. Pipe a whipped-cream rosette on top of each brownie and top with a chocolate espresso bean. Brownie mousse squares can be stored, refrigerated and loosely covered with plastic wrap, for up to 2 days.

MAKES 6 GENEROUS OR 9 AVERAGE SERVINGS

VALENCIA BROWNIE TORTE

A shiny, dark, bittersweet chocolate glaze cloaks this dense, rich, European-style dessert with an orange accent. We've used this recipe time and time again when we need a showstopping dessert for our most discriminating guests.

TORTE
1¼ cups (2½ sticks) unsalted
 butter, cut into pieces
5 ounces unsweetened
 chocolate, finely chopped
2 cups granulated sugar
5 large eggs, at room
 temperature, lightly beaten
2 tablespoons Grand Marnier
1 teaspoon vanilla extract
Grated rind of 1 large orange
1 cup all-purpose flour
¼ teaspoon salt
¾ cup pecans, finely chopped
 (about 3 ounces)

CANDIED ORANGE ZEST
1 large orange, washed, zest
 removed with a vegetable
 peeler
1 cup granulated sugar, plus
 additional sugar for rolling
1 cup water

GLAZE
⅔ cup heavy cream
8 ounces bittersweet or
 semisweet chocolate, finely
 chopped
2 tablespoons Grand Marnier

1. *Torte:* Position a rack in the center of the oven and preheat to 350°F. Line the bottom of a 9½-inch springform pan with a wax paper round.

2. In a large saucepan over low heat, melt butter. Add unsweetened chocolate and let stand 1 minute; whisk until smooth. Let stand 10 minutes, until tepid. Whisk in sugar. Whisk in eggs, then Grand Marnier, vanilla, and orange rind. Using a wooden spoon, stir in flour and salt. Stir in pecans.

3. Spread batter evenly into prepared pan and bake 50 to 60 minutes, until a toothpick inserted in the center comes out with a moist crumb. *Do not overbake.* Cool on a wire cake rack for 15 minutes. Run a knife around inside edge of pan to release brownie torte from sides. Remove sides of springform pan and invert onto the wire cake rack. Remove springform bottom and carefully peel off wax paper. Cool completely.

4. *Candied Orange Zest:* Cut the orange zest into strips ⅛-inch wide. In a small saucepan over medium heat, bring sugar and water to a boil, stirring constantly with a wooden spoon just until sugar dissolves. Add orange-zest strips and simmer for 20 minutes, until the strips are very tender. Drain the strips in a wire strainer and transfer them to a wire cake rack set over a wax paper–lined baking sheet. Using two forks, separate the strips and let them stand about 45 minutes, until tacky. Roll a few strips at a time in sugar, and transfer to a plate to dry completely.

5. *Glaze:* In a small saucepan over low heat, bring cream to a low simmer. Off heat, add chocolate and Grand Marnier and let stand 2 minutes; whisk until smooth. Transfer to a medium bowl and let stand 20 minutes, until tepid and slightly thickened.

6. Place the torte on the wire cake rack, the underside of the cake still facing up, on a wax paper–lined work surface. Pour the glaze over the top of the cake. Using a metal cake spatula, smooth the glaze over the top of the torte, letting excess glaze run down the sides. Use the spatula to pick up any excess glaze on the wax paper and to cover any bare spots. Garnish top edge of torte with candied orange zest. Transfer torte to a serving dish and refrigerate for 1 hour to set glaze. Torte can be stored, refrigerated and loosely covered with plastic wrap, for up to 3 days.

MAKES 12 TO 16 SERVINGS

LAYERED BROWNIE FUDGE PUDDING PARFAITS

The layered look is "in," especially in these fudgy pudding parfaits with alternating layers of chocolate pudding and fudgy brownie squares. You may use leftover trimmings from the St. Valentine's Strawberry Brownie Hearts (see Index), a half batch of Classic Chewy (see Index), or Traditional Fudgy Brownies (see Index), or your own favorite recipe.

PUDDING
⅓ cup granulated sugar
2 tablespoons cornstarch
⅛ teaspoon salt
2 cups half-and-half
6 ounces semisweet chocolate, finely chopped
2 large eggs, at room temperature
2 tablespoons unsalted butter, at room temperature

1 teaspoon vanilla extract

2 cups brownie trimmings (from St. Valentine's Strawberry Brownie Hearts; see Index), or ½ batch Classic Chewy or Traditional Fudgy Brownies (see Index), cut into ½-inch cubes

TOPPING
½ cup heavy cream
2 tablespoons confectioners' sugar
½ teaspoon vanilla extract

1. *Pudding:* In a heavy-bottomed medium saucepan, combine sugar, cornstarch, and salt. Add ⅓ cup half-and-half and whisk until cornstarch is dissolved. Add chopped chocolate and remaining 1⅔ cups half-and-half and cook over medium-low heat, stirring constantly with a wooden spoon, about 4 minutes, until mixture comes to a boil. Simmer mixture, stirring constantly, for 2 minutes. Remove pan from heat.

2. In a small bowl, whisk eggs until lightly beaten. Gradually add about 1 cup of hot chocolate mixture to the eggs, whisking constantly until blended. Whisk egg mixture back into saucepan. Return pan to very low heat and cook, stirring constantly, about 2 minutes, until slightly thickened. Do not let mixture come to a boil. Remove from heat and stir in butter and vanilla until butter is melted.

3. Spoon hot pudding into a large bowl, and place plastic wrap directly on top of the pudding's surface. Using a sharp knife, cut 2 to 3 slits in the plastic to allow steam to escape. Allow pudding to cool, then chill for at least 2 hours before serving.

4. *Topping:* In a chilled medium bowl, using a hand-held electric mixer set at high speed, beat cream until soft peaks begin to form. Add confectioners' sugar and vanilla and beat just until blended.

5. Spoon alternating layers of pudding and brownie squares into large goblets. Garnish each serving with a dollop of sweetened whipped cream.

MAKES 4 TO 6 GENEROUS SERVINGS

BROWNIE-CHIP WAFFLES

Any morning that we hear waffles sizzling on the waffle iron, we know it's going to be a great day. And when those waffles are made with cocoa, walnuts, and chocolate chips, we're ready to take on the world. (For true decadence, or to use these as a dinner dessert, serve them with vanilla ice cream and your favorite hot-fudge sauce.)

1 cup all-purpose flour
½ teaspoon baking soda
½ teaspoon salt
½ cup unsweetened nonalkalized cocoa powder, such as Hershey's
4 tablespoons (½ stick) unsalted butter, melted

¾ cup granulated sugar
2 large eggs, at room temperature
2 teaspoons vanilla extract
½ cup buttermilk or plain low-fat yogurt
2 ounces walnuts, finely chopped (about ½ cup)

⅓ cup miniature semisweet chocolate chips (about 2½ ounces)
Sliced fresh strawberries, for topping (optional)

1. Preheat a waffle iron. Sift flour, baking soda, and salt through a wire strainer onto a sheet of wax paper.

2. In a medium bowl, using a hand-held electric mixer set at low speed, beat cocoa and melted butter until smooth. Beat in sugar. Add eggs and vanilla and beat well. Alternately beat in buttermilk and flour mixture. Stir in walnuts and miniature chocolate chips.

3. Bake in waffle iron according to manufacturer's directions, about 3 to 4 minutes, or until the waffle batter stops steaming out of the sides of the waffle iron. Serve waffles warm with strawberries, if desired.

Variations: Fruit-flavored syrups are a delicious alternative to maple syrup. Or substitute sliced ripe bananas or fresh raspberries for strawberries.

MAKES 4 10-INCH WAFFLES

CHOCOLATE-DIPPED BROWNIE FINGERS

Arrange these in a spokelike pattern on a silver platter for an elegant teatime confection or a unique dessert alternative. Try dipping the ends in white chocolate or sprinkling chopped pistachios on the dark chocolate ends while still warm.

BROWNIE FINGERS
8 tablespoons (1 stick) unsalted butter, cut into pieces
3 ounces bittersweet chocolate, finely chopped
2 ounces unsweetened chocolate, finely chopped
2 large eggs, at room temperature

1 cup granulated sugar
2 tablespoons light corn syrup
1 teaspoon vanilla extract
1¼ cups all-purpose flour
¼ teaspoon baking soda
¼ teaspoon salt

GLAZE
½ cup heavy cream
8 ounces European bittersweet chocolate, finely chopped
3 ounces pecans, finely chopped (about ¾ cup)

1. *Brownie Fingers:* Position a rack in the center of the oven and preheat to 350°F. Line the bottom of a 10″ × 15″ jelly-roll pan with aluminum foil. Lightly butter and flour the foil, tapping out excess flour.

2. In a medium saucepan over low heat, melt butter. Off heat, add both chocolates and let stand 1 minute; whisk until smooth. Let stand 10 minutes, until tepid.

3. In a large bowl, using a hand-held electric mixer set at high speed, beat eggs and sugar for 2 to 3 minutes, until very light in color and texture. Beat in tepid chocolate mixture and corn syrup, then vanilla. Using a wooden spoon, stir in flour, baking soda, and salt, just until blended.

4. Spread batter evenly into prepared pan. Bake 8 to 10 minutes, just until a toothpick inserted in the center comes out with a moist crumb. Cool completely on a wire cake rack. Run a sharp knife around the inside edge of the pan to release brownie from sides of pan. Place a baking sheet on top of the brownie, and invert to remove brownie. Carefully peel off foil. Using a sharp knife, trim off any dried edges, if desired. Cut brownies into 48 rectangles, about ¾″ × 3½″ each.

5. *Glaze:* In a medium saucepan over low heat, bring cream to a low simmer. Off heat, add chocolate and let stand 1 minute; whisk until smooth. Transfer to a small, deep bowl and let stand 15 minutes, until tepid and slightly thickened.

6. Line a baking sheet with wax paper. Dip the bottom third of a brownie finger into the cooled glaze, scraping the bottom of the brownie finger on the lip of the bowl to remove excess chocolate. Place brownie finger on the wax paper–lined baking sheet. Repeat procedure with remaining brownie fingers. Sprinkle chopped pecans on glazed portion of each brownie finger. (Remaining glaze will keep, tightly covered and refrigerated, for up to 1 week. Reheat gently and use as a glaze or as an ice-cream topping.) Refrigerate for 15 minutes to set glaze.

MAKES 48 BROWNIE FINGERS

 # BROWNIE COOKIES

A brownie is a brownie, and a cookie is a cookie, but have you ever had a craving for a taste of both together? These cookies give you the best of both, with a crisp exterior surrounding a chewy chocolaty inside. And *they're a snap to prepare!*

2 ounces semisweet chocolate, coarsely chopped
8 tablespoons (1 stick) unsalted butter, at room temperature
1 cup granulated sugar
1 large egg, at room temperature
1 teaspoon vanilla extract

1½ cups all-purpose flour
½ teaspoon baking powder
½ teaspoon salt
½ cup miniature semisweet chocolate chips (about 3 ounces)
About 60 walnut halves, for garnish

1. Position a rack in the center of the oven and preheat to 350°F.

2. In the top part of a double boiler, over hot, not simmering, water, melt chocolate. Remove from heat and let stand 10 minutes, until tepid.

3. In a medium bowl, using a hand-held electric mixer set at high speed, beat butter and sugar for about 2 minutes, until light in color. Beat in egg and vanilla. Beat in melted chocolate. Using a wooden spoon, stir in flour, baking powder, and salt. Stir in miniature chocolate chips. Drop by rounded teaspoons onto an ungreased baking sheet. Press a walnut half into the top of each cookie, pressing down slightly to adhere.

4. Bake 10 to 12 minutes, until cookies are set and beginning to brown around the edges. Cool cookies on the ungreased baking sheet for 2 minutes, then transfer to a wire cake rack to cool completely. Repeat procedure with remaining cookie dough and walnut halves, using a cool baking sheet for each batch. (Cookies are always best baked one sheet at a time.)

MAKES ABOUT 60 COOKIES

INDEX